BIBLE 101

BIBLE GUIDES FOR LIFE

BIBLE 101

BARBOUR
PUBLISHING

Member of the Evangelical Christian Publishers Association

Printed in the United States of America.

CONTENTS

INTRODUCTION

The Bible is an overwhelming book. It's a big book jammed with information. It's filled with hundreds of stories and thousands of names. If you're like most people, you have a lot of questions:

"Where do I start?"
"How do I read the Bible?"
"How do I find help from the Bible when I really need it?"
"It's confusing and certain places are hard to read. How can I understand it?"
"Which Bible is best for me?"

Ever asked one of those? You're not alone. If you're like most people, you're met with a difficult choice: Do you try to dig in anyway, or forget about it and try another day? It's a tough choice because you know you should read the Bible, but it's certainly easier to put it aside for a rainy day.

Help has arrived.

Here's a book that will give you an informative, yet fun, overview of the Bible. You'll get your bearings and find your way through the Bible with new insight. The good news is that you don't need a PhD to get started; you only need to know where to find the answers. And this book is the place to start. Inside, you'll find:

 ## A Truckload of Clues

You'll learn tips from people who know the Bible inside and out. You'll find clues to help you get your own study under way.

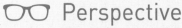 ## Perspective

We easily get caught up in the details of a book or story. To best understand the Bible, though, we sometimes need help looking at the whole picture. We'll help you take a step back.

Amazing Stories and Facts

The Bible is filled with interesting information. We've collected a few choice pieces for you to enjoy.

Important Reminders

Certain things are important to remember as you read your Bible. We've highlighted those for you.

The Bottom Line

We'll help you get beyond confusion by letting you know the most important stuff to remember.

Bible reading does not need to overwhelm or confuse you any longer. The questions you have are ready to be answered as you begin your guided tour of the Bible. There's just one thing you need to do: read this book. Feel free to read it your way: from cover to cover or skipping around to parts that interest you most. No matter how you read it, you'll find it's jammed with good advice, great ideas, and entertaining thoughts. So turn the page and start reading. . . . You'll be glad you did!

1

UNDERSTANDING THE BIBLE

Overview of the Bible

The Bible is the story of God reaching out to His creation, to people, to us. It opens with the creation of the earth and closes with the end of life as we know it. There are two main sections of the Bible. The first is the Old Testament, written before Christ came to earth. The second is the New Testament, written after Christ's birth, life, death, resurrection, and return to heaven.

OLD TESTAMENT

The Old Testament is made up of thirty-nine different "books." These books were inspired by God but written by different people in many walks of life and for many different purposes.

Some of the books are just one step beyond oral tradition. They are stories to be passed down to generations to come. Some of the books are almost legal documents; they are the rules and regulations of the day. Some are poetry, songs, hymns, proverbs. Some are sermons and prophecies.

The writers wrote out of their own abilities and context. It wasn't like they were saying to themselves, "I'm going to write a book and JUST MAYBE it will be included in the Bible one day." No. They wrote because an issue needed to be addressed or some history needed to be recorded. They responded to that need in the most effective way they could think of. God wrote the Bible through these writers as they responded to life around them.

Even though the Old Testament doesn't speak about Jesus like the Gospels do (the biographies of Jesus in the New Testament), the focus of the Old Testament is on the future coming of Christ. In the Old Testament Jesus is referred to as the Promised One, Messiah, Immanuel, the Redeemer. God's promise to Abraham included a promise that Jesus would come through Abraham's bloodline, the Jewish people. This is why the history of the Jewish people was so important: Jesus was climbing down that family tree. This is the significance of all the sacrifices you read about in the Old Testament: Jesus was promised as the ultimate sacrifice for sin.

NEW TESTAMENT

The second section of the Bible includes twenty-seven different documents or books. All of these books were written in the first hundred years after Jesus lived. Like the Old Testament, they were written by different people in different circumstances and for different reasons. Through God's leadership these documents were all pulled together as the collection we call the New Testament.

The New Testament is made up of books that tell the story of Jesus' life, death, and resurrection; the story of the church; and letters written to encourage those churches.

OLD TESTAMENT ORGANIZATION

Typically the Old Testament is broken down into these categories:

Books of Law

Written by Moses himself, these books tell about the beginning of the world and the Jewish nation. They tell history through stories and lists of things to remember.

Genesis	Leviticus	Deuteronomy
Exodus	Numbers	

Books of History

These books tell true stories of historical events. They span from when the Hebrews reentered Israel after leaving Egypt until they reentered Israel after their exile to Babylonia and Assyria. (Theirs is a rocky past.)

Joshua	1 Samuel	2 Kings	Ezra
Judges	2 Samuel	1 Chronicles	Nehemiah
Ruth	1 Kings	2 Chronicles	Esther

Books of Poetry

These books are more experiential. Some are stories, but they are not from an informational point of view so much as a grappling-with-life point of view.

Job	Proverbs	Song of Solomon
Psalms	Ecclesiastes	

Books of Prophecy

The prophets were the philosophers of the day, the street preachers, the Billy Grahams of ancient Israel. They told it like it was. In the process, through God's guidance, they also sometimes told it the way it would be when Christ came hundreds of years later. So they did do a little future-telling, but for the purpose of their people having hope and living clean lives within that hope.

Isaiah	Lamentations	Daniel
Jeremiah	Ezekiel	

The previous prophets are often called major prophets. We know more about them. They are more in the limelight of history. The lives of the prophets below were more obscure and their writings are shorter.

Hosea	Obadiah	Nahum	Haggai
Joel	Jonah	Habakkuk	Zechariah
Amos	Micah	Zephaniah	Malachi

NEW TESTAMENT ORGANIZATION

The New Testament is typically broken down into these categories:

The Gospels

These are biographies of the life of Jesus Christ.

Matthew	Luke
Mark	John

History
This is the story of the beginning of the New Testament church and the spread of the good news of Christ.

Acts

Letters (some people call these epistles)
These letters were written to the early churches. Some address the same problems in those first churches that we face today.

Romans	Ephesians	2 Thessalonians	Philemon
1 Corinthians	Philippians	1 Timothy	
2 Corinthians	Colossians	2 Timothy	
Galatians	1 Thessalonians	Titus	

The letters above were all written by Paul. The letters below are by a variety of writers.

Hebrews	1 Peter	1 John	3 John
James	2 Peter	2 John	Jude

Prophecy
This book is about the "end times" or the "Second Coming" (meaning, of Jesus). It could also be called apocalyptic (meaning, end of the world).

Revelation

ABBREVIATIONS OF BIBLE BOOKS

Gen.	Genesis	Josh.	Joshua
Ex.	Exodus	Judg.	Judges
Lev.	Leviticus	Ru.	Ruth
Num.	Numbers	1Sa.	1 Samuel
Deut.	Deuteronomy	2Sa.	2 Samuel

1Ki.	1 Kings	Ez.	Ezekiel
2Ki.	2 Kings	Dan.	Daniel
1Chr.	1 Chronicles	Hos.	Hosea
2Chr.	2 Chronicles	Joel	Joel
Ezr.	Ezra	Am.	Amos
Neh.	Nehemiah	Ob.	Obadiah
Est.	Esther	Jnh.	Jonah
Job	Job	Mic.	Micah
Ps.	Psalms	Na.	Nahum
Pr.	Proverbs	Hab.	Habakkuk
Eccl.	Ecclesiastes	Zep.	Zephaniah
Song.	Song of Solomon	Hag.	Haggai
Isa.	Isaiah	Zec.	Zechariah
Jer.	Jeremiah	Mal.	Malachi
Lam.	Lamentations		

Mt.	Matthew	1Ti.	1 Timothy
Mk.	Mark	2Ti.	2 Timothy
Lk.	Luke	Tit.	Titus
Jn.	John	Phm.	Philemon
Ac.	Acts	Heb.	Hebrews
Rom.	Romans	Jas.	James
1Cor.	1 Corinthians	1Pe.	1 Peter
2Cor.	2 Corinthians	2Pe.	2 Peter
Gal.	Galatians	1Jn.	1 John
Eph.	Ephesians	2Jn.	2 John
Php.	Philippians	3Jn.	3 John
Col.	Colossians	Jude	Jude
1Th.	1 Thessalonians	Rev.	Revelation
2Th.	2 Thessalonians		

The Story of the Bible

The story of the Bible is the story of God reaching out to build a relationship with the people of the earth. It is a simple straight line between God's heart and ours.

If it sometimes seems difficult, it's because the Bible was written in another culture, in another time, in another language. It had to be translated from Greek and Hebrew into more modern languages, including English. But there is another whole translation that has to happen and that is a cultural translation. We have to understand the events described in the Bible in terms of their significance to that time.

THE STORY

As most people probably know, the Bible opens with the story of the creation of the world. God created two people, Adam and Eve. He gave them a lovely environment with one guideline. In responding to this guideline, they had the choice to walk with God or to walk their own way. They chose to walk their own way. Each one of us since then has chosen to walk our own way as well.

Adam and Eve had children, who had children, who had children, and so on. Each generation ignored God more than the generation before. God regretted, in so many words, that He had even made people. By Noah's generation, God recognized him as the one man who still had faith in God. The flood came and destroyed the earth. God started over with just Mr. and Mrs. Noah, their three sons, and the three sons' wives. (If this is sounding familiar, remember that this was way before the series with Fred MacMurray, *My Three Sons*, and the neighborhood was a lot sparser.)

Noah's children had children, who had children, who had children, and so on, but things just didn't get a whole lot better. People still went their own ways. At this point God made a special covenant or "relationship based on a promise" with a man named Abraham. God told Abraham to pick up and move to a place called Canaan and to settle there, no questions asked (which Abraham did). God promised Abraham that he would be the father of a great nation. This is where the Jewish nation comes from, this very promise.

The wild thing about this part of the story is that Abraham and his wife were very old and had never been able to have children. Think about the faith it took for them to believe God's promise. They did falter some, but in the end a son, Isaac, was born to Abraham and Sarah. He was a miracle baby and the beginning of a people who would have a special relationship with God.

Isaac and his wife, Rebekah, had twin sons, Jacob and Esau. Their son, Jacob, had twelve sons who became the twelve tribes of Israel from whom all Jewish people descend.

Jacob and his twelve sons and their families moved to Egypt to escape famine. They were in Egypt for many generations and eventually became a nation of slaves there. It was discrimination to the tenth degree. It got so bad that the king of Egypt ordered all Jewish boy babies killed just to provide some control over the population. That is precisely when Moses, the great Hebrew leader, was born.

After Adam and Noah, Moses is about the most famous guy in the Old Testament. Moses confronted the king of Egypt and stole his people away (after some helpful coercion from God Himself). Moses was to lead his people back to the land that Abraham had settled and that Jacob had left to come to Egypt. The land was called Israel, a name that God gave to Jacob.

After two years of traveling like gypsies, the Jewish people got to the border of Israel but were too scared to cross over into their land. Understand that by that time other people had settled there. The Jewish people were going to have to do battle to take over their property. They cowered. They disbelieved God's promise, even though He had led them miraculously out of Egypt and through the desert. They retreated and wandered through the desert again.

About forty years later, when a new generation had arisen, they tried again to

LAW

During Moses' time, God gave His people laws and rules. These laws showed how sinful people are and that God required blood as a penalty for sin (important to remember when you read about the life of Jesus).

enter the land under a leader named Joshua. This time they reclaimed their land. But, and listen well, they didn't run everyone else out of it. This simple fact lays the groundwork for the whole rest of the Old Testament.

You see, the reason the Jewish people were supposed to run EVERYONE ELSE out of the land is because EVERYONE ELSE worshipped false gods. During their travels God had given the Jewish people the Ten Commandments, which began with "You shall have no other gods before me." You know how human nature is. If they let idol worship stay in their land, eventually they would be influenced by it.

And that's exactly what happened.

The rest of the Old Testament really revolves around Israel's struggle to worship God and only God. They would drift into idol worship and then a prophet would preach to them and call them back to obedience. They would drift again and a good judge would rise up and chase out their enemies, and they would follow God. They would drift again and a good king would come into power, and they'd return to God's ways. Back and forth, back and forth. Drifting and returning, drifting and returning.

They were taken into captivity finally by the Assyrians and the Babylonians, who were later taken over by the Persians, who let the Jewish people return to their home only to start the whole cycle over again.

But all the way through this story, from the first time Adam chose his own way, to the last time the Jewish nation drifted into idol worship, there was a promise. The promise always started with an understood, "One day. . ." In the garden of Eden this promise was to the serpent: One day, "he will crush your head, and you will strike his heel" (Genesis 3:15). Later this promise was to Abraham: One day, "all peoples on earth will be blessed through you" (Genesis 12:3). Later the promise came through the prophets: One day, "the Lord himself will give you a sign: The virgin will conceive and give birth to a son, and will call him Immanuel" (Isaiah 7:14).

All the way through the story, thus far, there was the promise of one coming who would fix what had been broken when people chose their own way rather than God's. That's what Jesus' life is all about. The Old Testament asked a question: How can we be right with God since we've chosen our own way? The New Testament answered it: through the life, death, and resurrection of Jesus Christ.

The New Testament opens with the birth of Jesus. He was born miraculously to a virgin. He was God, having put humanity on so that He could go through our experience and give Himself up for our sins. He lived thirty years before He really started a public ministry. For three years then he traveled, preached, worked miracles, and apprenticed twelve guys who could carry on His work. He enraged the religious leaders of His day because (1) He claimed to be God and (2) He confronted their hypocrisy. He said to them in so many words, "God is not about your little dos and don'ts. God is about how you live your lives and connect with Him and love other people."

At the age of thirty-three, Jesus was sentenced to death. It was really a political frame-up instigated by the religious leaders. But Jesus accepted His fate because this was what He came here to do, to die innocently and take the place of each of us who is not innocent, so that we could be right with God.

 JESUS CHRIST

Christ's life, death, and resurrection are what the first four books of the New Testament are about in detail. The rest of the New Testament is really a record of how Jesus' followers sorted through what had happened; how they regrouped and moved ahead. They organized themselves, their work, their ministry. They preached. They established churches. They went out on missionary journeys. They wrote letters. They apprenticed younger men and women in faith. They did whatever they could to get this news out: God has made a way for us to be right with Himself! He came here and gave His life. He died so that sin could be punished and we could have a relationship with Him.

That is the story of the Bible. In little pieces it sometimes seems too much to take in. It's not so difficult, though, when you understand that it is all a record of God befriending humanity even though He is perfect and we are not. What He asks of us is that we believe in Him and the sacrifice He made for us enough to choose His way rather than our own self-destructive way.

Jesus died on crossbeams of wood. This kind of death is called a crucifixion. It is a painful and agonizing execution, but typical for that period of history.

Three days later, Jesus returned from the dead. He met with His grief-stricken followers. He said some good-byes. Then He "ascended" or went up into heaven. It seemed, in some ways, unbelievable. That's why it takes faith to believe it.

Timeline of the Bible

To put everything in context, here is a timeline with some key events. Keep in mind, there are a lot of differing opinions about the dates. In fact, with a lot of these events we don't know the exact date. For some, we know of a range that could be as short as 300 years or as long as 1,000 years. In the list below we have often rounded to the nearest century. So remember the figures we've included are ballpark figures (no, not ballpark franks, ballpark figures). The purpose of this list is just to understand what came first and what came later, to get an order of thought going.

AROUND ABOUT...	THIS IS WHAT HAPPENS...
The beginning of time	God creates the world. Adam and Eve begin their family.
8000 B.C.	God saves Noah and his family from the flood.
3000 B.C.	The pyramids are built in Egypt.
2000 B.C.	God makes Abraham father of the Jewish nation by giving him Isaac, his son.
1800 B.C.	Joseph, Isaac's grandson, is sold into Egypt. Joseph's family's descendants become slaves in Egypt eventually and need God to set them free.
1400 B.C.	Moses leads the Hebrew people out of Egypt. This is called the Exodus.
1350 B.C.	After Moses' death Joshua leads the Hebrews in conquering the land God had promised them.
1300 B.C.	After Joshua's death the Hebrews are led by judges, very wise men and women who helped settle disagreements and make good choices. Ruth lived during this time.
1000 B.C.	God gives Israel their first kings: King Saul, King David, and King Solomon.

950 B.C.	The temple at Jerusalem is built.
900 B.C.	King Solomon dies. The kingdom is divided into Israel (10 northern tribes) and Judah (remaining southern tribes).
850 B.C.	Elijah is a leader and a prophet. His successor is Elisha.
800 B.C.	Isaiah, Joel, Micah, Obadiah, and Nahum prophesy to Judah while Hosea, Amos, and Jonah prophesy to Israel.
770 B.C.	First Greek Olympic Games.
750 B.C.	Rome becomes a city.
600 B.C.	The people of Judah are taken captive into Babylon. The prophets during this time are Jeremiah, Ezekiel, and Daniel.
500 B.C.	The first exiles return to Jerusalem and begin to rebuild.
450 B.C.	The rebuilding of the temple is complete. The ruler at this time is Cyrus the Persian. The Jewish leadership is Ezra and Nehemiah. The prophets are Haggai and Zechariah.
425 B.C.	Queen Esther is crowned in Persia. (A Jewish queen of Persia?)
400 B.C.	Last book of the Old Testament, Malachi, is complete. This book closes with the prophecy of the coming of John the Baptist, Jesus' cousin, which is the event that opens the New Testament.
250 B.C.	The Septuagint is written. This is a Greek translation of the Old Testament. Greek was the common language of that time, so this was a big deal. Jesus and His disciples probably used this translation.
150 B.C.	The Maccabean revolt. A dad and five brothers lead a revolt against an evil Syrian ruler. Judas, the eldest son, leads the Jewish nation into a time of prosperity.
100 B.C.	Julius Caesar is assassinated and Augustus Caesar becomes the new ruler (he is the one who ordered the census that caused Joseph and very pregnant Mary to travel to Bethlehem where Jesus was born).

BEGINNING OF A.D. TIME—JESUS IS BORN.

A.D. 30	Jesus is crucified or assassinated and miraculously returns to life. After He returns to heaven, the Holy Spirit arrives at a time that we now call "Pentecost."
A.D. 60	Paul writes his early letters to the churches.
A.D. 65	Mark's Gospel, then Matthew's Gospel, then Luke's Gospel and Acts are written.
A.D. 70	Jerusalem is destroyed again.
A.D. 80	Mt. Vesuvius erupts in Italy.

A.D. 85	John's Gospel is written. Paul is making his missionary journeys.
A.D. 90	The individual churches start sharing Paul's letters with each other.
A.D. 100	The four Gospels are circulated together as a collection.
A.D. 120	All thirteen of Paul's letters are pulled together as a collection. (We now call these the Pauline Epistles.)
A.D. 140	A man named Marcion puts together a Bible that rejects the Old Testament and rewrites a lot of the New Testament. This motivates the church leaders to make a decision about what books make up the New Testament.
A.D. 145	The Church stands against Marcion and recognizes all the books of the New Testament. This Testament was almost identical to ours.
A.D. 400	An official council acknowledges what had already been proven as people experienced the power of God's Word: The twenty-seven books that we know today as the New Testament are true and inspired by God.

Literary Aspects of the Bible

We know the Bible now in rearview. We can look back from our vantage point through history and see how it all came to be. But in order to really understand the Bible, we have to be able to look from the perspective of the writers, as they were experiencing life.

They didn't know that their work would one day be collected into the Holy Scriptures. They weren't thinking they were going to be on a bestseller list. They were like we are: driven by the issues they felt passionately about.

- Moses wrote because he didn't want the history of God's provision to be forgotten. He wrote in the style in which he felt comfortable—narrative. He just told the facts as they happened.

- David didn't set out to write psalms that could be translated into today's praise music. He just wrote about the parts of life that he was processing, and they became a part of Psalms.

- Jeremiah's heart was broken because his people continued, over and over, to fall away from God. Jeremiah knew that this would lead to their own destruction. So he pulled out all the stops to convince them to turn back. He used metaphors. He used dramatic language.

He forecast the consequences of their behavior. His style of writing poured out of who he was and how he communicated.

Because the Bible was written by so many different authors, it is written in a lot of different literary styles. We read each book best when we understand the perspective of the author. Here are some categories that might help.

HISTORICAL NARRATIVES

Genesis, Exodus, Numbers, and the Gospels are some prime examples of historical narratives. They teach us about history but not just the facts of history. They tell us the story of history, the people, the places, the marriages, the family conflicts. Historical narratives were one step above oral tradition. They were the way history was passed along.

POETRY

Poetry is poetry. There is nothing else like it. It is to be experienced. It is to be savored, rolled around in your mind, and digested bit by bit. It is life's encounters recorded through one writer's perspective and applied as it was meaningful for him. Hebrew poetry didn't rhyme like contemporary poetry often does. It was called poetry because of its structure and style. Psalms, Proverbs, Ecclesiastes, and Song of Solomon are classic poetry books, perhaps even poetic philosophy books that cut a slice of life and place it on a plate with presentation as a primary concern.

PROPHECIES

A bulk of the Old Testament is made up of prophetic passages. Isaiah through Malachi (the last book) are prophetic books. These prophets spoke to their own culture, as well as to the future. When they were written, the only Bible to speak of was the Book of the Law (the first five books of the Old Testament). Today when we think of hearing God speak or of Him revealing Himself, we think of the wealth of His words we have in the Bible. Back then, though, they were still waiting for fresh news from God. They got it through the prophets. From our vantage point, looking back, we can see that many of the prophecies have come true ("The virgin will conceive. . ."). Looking ahead we learn from the prophets that there is still much of God's master plan to experience.

TEACHING PASSAGES

There are many passages that are specifically meant to teach us. They aren't giving us a story and letting us draw our conclusions. They aren't poetry or narratives. They are in-your-face, this-is-how-it-is-and-will-be truth. They are intended to train us and to teach us, to inform us and to form us. The Gospels are filled with teaching passages. Some of the epistles include them as well.

PARABLES

The Gospels include many of Jesus' parables. The importance of these passages was not in the facts of the story. The importance was in the principles underlying the story line. When we read the story of the woman who continues to knock on someone's door until they answer, it's not important what the woman wanted or whether a woman would have knocked on a door that long. What is important is that when we seek answers from God, we have a better chance of finding them the longer we persevere.

EPISTLES OR LETTERS

Most of the New Testament is written in the form of letters, personal letters to churches and to people. We need not be put off by the personal information at the beginning and the end. And we need to search out why the writer wrote about specific issues. Was he responding to very specific situations and sometimes specific letters he had received? We need to sift through what was specific to that church situation and then draw principles from it that we can apply to us today.

CABLE STATION SYNOPSIS

It might be easier to understand the whole literary-style thing if you think about cable TV stations. TV is going the way of radio these days in that each station is finding a niche or a format. Their shows all fit within that format. Except for the few traditional networks, the cooking shows are on a channel about cooking. The sports shows are on a channel about sports. If the books of the Bible were assigned to a cable channel, they might divide up like this.

Television for Women

Esther, Ruth, and Song of Solomon: These would definitely fit in with "chick" TV. It's not that they don't have eternal truths for everyone tucked away in their story lines, but the strong female characters are just the kind of people who inspire other women.

Science Fiction or Psychic Channel

Prophecy: Even though the prophets of the Old Testament and the writer of the book of Revelation didn't always know it, they were often writing about the future. Since God was in charge, though, they were always accurate. Since they didn't have telephones and billing charges, they broadcast in person free of charge.

Real-Life TV

Joshua, Judges, Ezra, Nehemiah: These books are historical narratives, but they are full of action, suspense, and adventure. If they had a cameraman running behind, you'd better believe we'd be watching them, whether they fuzzed out the Philistine faces or not.

Advice TV

Proverbs: Everyday wisdom to make decisions by.

History Channel or Even the News

1 and 2 Samuel, 1 and 2 Kings, 1 and 2 Chronicles, and Acts: These books would be prime targets for who, what, when, where. They record not only what happened, but often what impact it had on the culture and what motivations were involved.

Music Station

Psalms: Video programming has never seen the likes of the Psalms. (Just what kind of spin would you put on Psalm 18? Talk about special effects.)

Biography Channel

Ezra, Nehemiah, Job, and the Gospels: All these books give the story of one man's life. Truth be known, the Gospels could fit into a lot of channels because, in telling the story of Christ's life, they run the gamut from parables to miracles to history to science fiction. (They'd probably even make it to public access.)

Christian TV

The epistles or letters of the New Testament: These were letters written specifically to churches or Christian leaders dealing with real issues and encouraging them in their faith. Put a host in front of a microphone and let him go.

Recommended Reading

There are many books that can help you understand the Bible more. You can often find them at a Christian bookstore in your area. Usually these books are gathered under a heading like "Bible Study Helps" or "The Bible." Here are a few different kinds, or formats, of books....

COMMENTARIES

Commentaries usually cover a portion of the Bible, maybe a certain book or section. They take apart that portion of the Bible, verse by verse, and give you as much information about each word and phrase and as much background information as possible. New commentaries are written all the time, but there are many older commentaries that are still useful.

BIBLE DICTIONARIES

Bible dictionaries list both people and objects that are listed in the Bible. They often give information about the culture of the Bible (for instance, what harps looked like in the time of David), as well as biographical history on people listed in the Bible. If you are reading along in the Bible and there is a word you don't understand (like *lyre* or *pomegranate*), a Bible dictionary is a good place to look.

BIBLE STUDIES

Some Bible studies are based on a certain book of the Bible. Often these Bible studies are written to be used with a group, so discussion questions are included. They are not usually expensive and are often small paperback books.

CONCORDANCES

Concordances are similar to dictionaries in that you can look up specific words. For each word you look up, though, all you will find in a concordance is, maybe, a little about the origin of the word and a list of the places in the Bible where that word is mentioned. Now that there are so many translations of the Bible, you need to pay attention to whether your concordance is based on a certain translation. The King James Version of the Bible often uses very different language from the New International Version or the Living Bible. A concordance based on one version might not be very helpful for another.

BIBLE HANDBOOKS

A Bible handbook often lists the books of the Bible in the order they appear. It then will give you background information about that book, its main characters, and its context in history.

STUDY BIBLES

You may have noticed, if you've looked at Bibles lately, that many Bibles come packed with study helps. They may have their own concordances, or lists of famous passages, or a dictionary in the back. If you are about to buy a Bible, take time to look through its Bible study helps.

BIBLE ENCYCLOPEDIAS

You can most likely figure this out since you probably know the difference between a dictionary and an encyclopedia. A Bible encyclopedia will list fewer words than a Bible dictionary, but it will give you more information about the words it lists.

SOME SUGGESTIONS

Bruce and Stan's Guide to the Bible, Bruce Bickel and Stan Jantz, Harvest House, 1998

Pictorial Introduction to the Bible, William S. Deal, Hendrickson Publishers, 1997

The New International Dictionary of the Bible, J. D. Douglas and Merrill C. Tenney, eds., Zondervan, 1987

Strong's Exhaustive Concordance, Abingdon Press

Unger's Bible Dictionary, Merrill F. Unger, Moody Press

Vine's Expository Dictionary of Old and New Testament Words, W. E. Vine, Fleming H. Revell Co.

Life Application Bible, Tyndale House Publishers

2

HOW TO READ
YOUR BIBLE

How to Study the Bible

WHAT'S THE BIG DEAL?

Why do you need this book to tell you how to read the Bible? In fact, why are hundreds of books published for the same reason? If you are like most people, and you probably are because you're reading this book, you've struggled to read or study the Bible. Do some of these comments sound familiar?

- "I know I should read my Bible, but I don't know where to start."
- "Every New Year's I make a resolution to read through my Bible. I do pretty well for a while, but then I hit Leviticus. What's the use of reading something I don't understand?"
- "So much of the Bible doesn't seem to be relevant to my life."
- "Whenever I read my Bible, I come up with more questions than answers! It's too frustrating!"

Okay, we know it's difficult to make Bible study a priority. So why bother? We'll list some good reasons for you. Read them carefully and slowly. (This is our tricky way of getting you started.)

All Scripture is God-breathed and is useful for teaching, rebuking, correcting and training in righteousness, so that the servant of God may be thoroughly equipped for every good work.
2 TIMOTHY 3:16–17

The law of the LORD is perfect, refreshing the soul. The statutes of the LORD are trustworthy, making wise the simple. The precepts of the LORD are right, giving joy to the heart. The commands of the LORD are radiant, giving light to the eyes. The fear of the LORD is pure, enduring forever. The decrees of the LORD are firm, and all of them are righteous. They are more precious than gold, than much pure gold; they are sweeter than honey, than honey from the honeycomb. By them your servant is warned; in keeping them there is great reward.

PSALM 19:7–11

Keep this Book of the Law always on your lips; meditate on it day and night, so that you may be careful to do everything written in it. Then you will be prosperous and successful.

JOSHUA 1:8

We also can look to the example of Jesus Christ. He depended on the spiritual disciplines of prayer and studying the scriptures to help Him stand firm, resist temptation, and obey the will of His Father. Knowing we would need these spiritual habits even more than He did, He commanded us to follow in His footsteps.

All this leads us to conclude that regular Bible study should be one of our top priorities. But it's one thing to know that we should read the Bible; it's quite another thing to do it regularly. Most people need help getting started and even more help to keep going. These few pages will offer practical, easy-to-follow advice that will help you in your quest.

HELPFUL HINTS FOR GETTING STARTED

Are you intimidated by lofty theological terms? Use a modern translation of the Bible, such as the New Living Translation, New Century Version, or *GOD'S WORD*.

Differentiate between the actual Bible and all of the study helps you use to assist you in understanding and applying biblical truths. Nowadays, many Bibles have notes scattered throughout the text written by fallible authors. Be careful not to read those sections as "gospel truth." Only the Bible text itself is inspired by God and carries His authority.

Pray before you begin to read your Bible. God's Spirit plays an integral role in revealing the truths of scripture to us. Invite His Spirit to open your eyes and heart to spiritual truth in God's Word. Remember the promise in 1 John 2:27 NLT: "But you have received the Holy Spirit, and he lives within you, so you don't need anyone to teach you what is true. For the Spirit teaches you everything you need to know, and what he teaches is true—it is not a lie. So just as he has taught you, remain in fellowship with Christ."

Does your mind wander? Read the Bible aloud as you study. This will help you remember and retain what you read much better than reading silently.

Accountability can help! Find a friend who is willing to keep you accountable to read the Bible, to challenge you when you falter, to encourage you when you feel like giving up. It helps to choose someone who wants the relationship to be mutual; otherwise you could begin to resent that person's help.

However you do it, read your Bible. Daily Bible study produces a level of spiritual growth and communion with God that nothing else can provide. The more you saturate your life with God's Word, the more intimate your relationship with God will become, and the stronger you will stand against temptation.

WHAT'S FOR DINNER?

Reading your Bible is like feeding yourself spiritually. And there is a smorgasbord of choices for you. As you read through this list, think about where you are in your spiritual journey and what type of personality you have. Different people gravitate toward different Bible study plans. Choose one that suits who you are and where you are in life right now. Maybe next year a different plan will appeal to you. Even in spiritual things, variety is the spice of life!

An Appetizer—If you're just beginning to develop this spiritual discipline, start with a simple, easily digestible diet. Begin with some of the most well-known passages, such as John 14; Romans 8; Psalm 23; Psalm 150; 1 John 1; John 10; 1 Corinthians 15; Hebrews 11; Luke 24; Matthew 5–7; and Psalm 1. When you have studied these passages, choose to read through a whole book. Try John, then Acts, 1 John, Romans, and Ephesians. Some good beginner books in the Old Testament include Genesis, Psalms,

Proverbs, Esther, and Isaiah. After you have read several books of the Bible, you may be ready to read through the entire Bible.

The Sampler Platter—One-year Bibles arrange all of scripture into 365 daily readings, combining selections from the Old and New Testaments, Psalms, and Proverbs for every day. Choose this option if you are committed to reading at least fifteen to twenty minutes each day and like a variety in your spiritual diet. Just a note: These plans can be adjusted to stretch out over two or three years for less ambitious readers.

Good Ol' Meat and Potatoes—Start at page one and read through the whole Bible (not all in one sitting, of course). Many people follow this simplest of plans even though so many Bible study helps and plans are available at Christian bookstores. This schedule works for people who want to read straight through scripture and can make it through the books that are more challenging to read.

The Daily Special—Follow a Bible study guide, either one that studies a topic of interest to you or one focused on one of the books of the Bible. Many people prefer to work on a study guide with a small group, which offers the added benefit of accountability.

HOW TO STAY IN IT FOR THE LONG HAUL

Most of us know the challenge of beginning a new diet program or exercise regime. The beginning is always the hardest. It's during those first few weeks that most of us lose interest or get discouraged by lack of results. But if we fight the urge to give up and keep with it, our minds and bodies get into the sync of the new routine. The same is true for Bible study.

How to Apply the Bible

The Bible isn't an encyclopedia or a novel. It's not just a bound set of facts and figures, plotlines and poems. God gave us the Bible to communicate Himself to us and to *change our lives* through that knowledge of Him.

BANDAGES AND BIBLE VERSES

It's like this: If you cut your hand, it needs a bandage. If that bandage is sitting there on the counter in its wrapper, it's not doing any good. The bandage only helps when you *apply* it to the wound.

We are all wounded—we don't always do what's right even when we really, really want to. God has given us a bandage with a built-in antibiotic called the truth of God. It's up to us to apply that bandage and find the healing that is there.

So what does it mean to *apply* the Bible? It means to take it personally. If the Bible says that God desires our obedience, it's up to us to say, "Then how should I obey?" If the Bible tells a story about a man who is unmerciful and lives to regret it, it's up to us to say, "How do I measure up in the 'merciful' category?" If a Bible passage commends God's very nature and lavishes compliments on Him, then it's up to us to say, "Do I worship God this way? Am I this caught up in His power and majesty?"

THE DIGESTION PROCESS

Journaling is an effective tool for many people in "digesting" God's Word. Writing down portions of God's Word helps it take root in your heart. Recording your thoughts, insights, decisions, and prayers during and after your time of Bible study will help you remember and apply what you have learned throughout your day.

IT TAKES SOME DIGGING

The first step to applying a verse or a passage of the Bible is to ask yourself, "What kind of passage is this?"

- Is it a story? (If so, you'll learn from someone's example or a conversation.)
- Is it a teaching passage, like a sermon or a letter? (If so, you'll probably need to respond to a direct command or lesson.)
- Is it an artistic passage, like a song or a poem? (If so, you'll probably be inspired by the thoughts of someone else to feel or think differently about God.)

You'll have to ask yourself, "Does this passage mean I should do exactly what the person in this story or passage is doing?" Sometimes that's easy—for instance: "Therefore receive one another, just as Christ also received us, to the glory of God" (Romans 15:7 NKJV). This verse is from a teaching passage, a letter from Paul to a church. It is easy to see the truth we should apply. *Give people a break because God gave you a break. Accept them as they are.*

CHANGING LIVES

There is a Bible verse in Hebrews that says, *"For the word of God is alive and active* [not just words on a page].

"Sharper than any double-edged sword [very powerful and very adept at its task], *it penetrates even to dividing soul and spirit, joints and marrow* [it reaches inside of us where we think and feel and pray, where people aren't watching].

"It judges the thoughts and attitudes of the heart [it shows us ourselves, the way we really are and asks us to become more]" (Hebrews 4:12).

If the Bible is not changing us, then it's not doing what God intended it to do. If we are not applying the Bible to our lives, then we are not allowing the Bible to change us.

Other times it's a little more complex. Let's say you read the story in which God tells Abraham to sacrifice his only son. God stops Abraham before he does it and commends his willingness to give up his most important thing (Genesis 22). Now, *watch closely*: When you apply this passage, it has nothing to do with how you treat your children. It has to do with how you prioritize your life. Are there things so important that you couldn't give them up even if God asked you to?

See? Ask yourself what the bottom line is. Then ask, "How should my life be different in light of this?" Then *make the change*. That's when the Bible has been applied.

WANT MORE INFORMATION?
CHECK OUT THESE RESOURCES

- Paul Kent, *Know Your Bible* (Uhrichsville, OH: Barbour Publishing, 2008).
- Robert M. West, *How to Study the Bible* (Uhrichsville, OH: Barbour Publishing, 2007).
- John Beck, *Understand Your Bible* (Uhrichsville, OH: Barbour Publishing, 2011).

How to Have a Quiet Time

GET GOING

Ever heard the saying "No time is better than the present"? It certainly applies to starting the habit of reading God's Word and praying (some people call this "having a quiet time").

You may have a lot of questions about the right way to do it. Look through our "Q and A" section to find some practical help.

Another great way to find answers is to ask people you respect. If you know people who read the Bible regularly, ask them what they do to maintain their motivation. God wants us to learn from one another.

Q AND A

1. When should I read my Bible?

Choose a time of day when your mind is alert and fresh. For some, the best time is early morning; for others, it's before bedtime. Another option is to divide your quiet time into shorter segments so you can start your day with God and end your day with God.

2. I'm having trouble making the time. What should I do?

Consistency and accountability are keys to your long-term success. It doesn't matter so much when you read your Bible as long as you set aside the same time every day to do it. Regular times of Bible study and prayer must be scheduled into your routine or they'll rarely happen. Also, most people find it helpful to have someone keep them accountable. It's harder to neglect your quiet time if you know someone will call you on it.

3. What kind of Bible should I use?

The many options of Bible translations and versions can be intimidating. We've included in this book a section on special Bibles and translations. Reading through those pages will give you a better understanding of what is available on the market and what each different translation has to offer.

Once you make your decision, stick with that version. Although there is value in comparing translations, consistently using the same translation will make it easier for you to become familiar with your Bible and memorize key verses.

4. How should I read my Bible?

First, approach your time with God with the right attitude. Think about the privilege of holding God's Word in your hands—many people throughout the years have died to protect it. It's a book that holds all the spiritual insight you need for life. John 6:63 says, "The Spirit gives life; the flesh counts for nothing. The words I have spoken to you—they are full of the Spirit and life."

Second, always acknowledge your need for Bible study. Expect to learn from God each time you read His Word. "Crave pure spiritual milk, so that by it you may grow up in your salvation, now that you have tasted that the Lord is good" (1 Peter 2:2–3).

Third, study your Bible with an open heart and mind. Give the Holy Spirit free rein to call you to repentance and change. Don't waste your time reading it if you don't plan to obey.

Fourth, do all you can to keep your devotional time interesting and alive.

Reading aloud can help you concentrate. Varying the length of passage you read each day can add interest. Be creative! Do whatever it takes to maintain your commitment.

Fifth, read your Bible faithfully. The more you devote yourself to prayer and Bible study, the more God will teach you.

5. How should I pray?

William Carey wrote, "Prayer—secret, fervent, believing prayer—lies at the root of all personal godliness."

Keep in mind that prayer is a learned discipline. Seek to learn all you can about it and you'll find it spilling over into every aspect of your life.

6. Should I do anything else besides read my Bible and pray?

Your quiet time can be enriched by worship. Meditate on the psalms, or some of your favorite hymns or praise choruses, to help you articulate your praise to God.

3

BIBLE CULTURE

Food and Clothes in Bible Times

POPCORN AND FIGS

Grain was the universal food source in Bible times; in fact, grain was so valuable, it was often used as money. Because it could be dried, grain outlasted most other sources of food, such as dairy products, meats, and vegetables.

While the men planted, tended, and harvested the crops, the women and children worked to prepare the family's meals. For example, corn seeds needed to be sorted to remove any poisonous kernels, then either popped on a hot griddle or ground into cornmeal to make flat corn cakes.

In addition to grain crops, grapes, olives, and figs were readily grown in the Holy Land. Grapes were crushed and fermented for drinking. Olives were crushed for their oil, which was used for cooking, cleaning, lighting, and medicinal purposes. Figs also added a nice variety to people's diets.

WEATHER PERMITTING

Rain and sun. Chemical fertilizers and pesticides. High-tech machinery. Quality control and safety inspections. Storage, refrigeration, and transportation. Farmers today rely on all of these things to grow, harvest, and distribute their crops. Now imagine what it would be like for farmers if they could depend on nothing more than the natural elements, unpredictable as they are.

Most people in Bible times relied almost completely on their own crops for survival. If the weather conditions varied or insect activity increased, famine could set in. Several extreme famines are recorded in scripture, such as the seven years of famine in Israel and all the surrounding nations during Joseph's lifetime (Genesis 41:53). God sometimes used famine to draw His people back to Himself (2 Kings 6:33).

"THAT'S NOT ON THE MENU"

Jewish law labeled some foods "unclean," meaning no Jew could eat them without being defiled and considered unclean in the eyes of God. The list of forbidden food included camels, rabbits, badgers, pigs, reptiles, and certain

TYPICAL MEAL

If you were a Jew living in Bible times, what would be likely to greet you at the dinner table?

Beverages. Water was the most common beverage. Wine was also used in the form of new wine or fermented wine. Milk was also a staple, from either cows or goats.

Sack lunches. A worker often took his lunch in a hollowed-out loaf of bread, filled with cheese or olives. Dessert may have been dried figs that had been boiled in a form of molasses.

Meals. Jews in Bible Times often ate just two meals a day. The first meal could be anytime from morning till noon, after the work of the morning. The evening meal came when the day's work ended. It was usually the main meal of the Hebrews.

Bread. This was a necessity at every meal. It was usually eaten warm and seldom by itself. Because they didn't use utensils, the bread was used to pick up the meat from a common dish on the table.

Each meal probably contained grains, vegetables, fruits, and animal foods (meat), not in steaks but chopped up and mixed with rice or served in gravy.

birds including eagles, vult-ures, falcons, owls, and bats. These dietary laws protected God's people from disease and contamination as well as set them apart from other people in the world. Although these restrictions aren't considered applicable to Christians today, the principle of maintaining holiness and difference from the world is more than relevant to modern-day believers.

WEATHER AND WEALTH RULE THE FASHION SCENE

In Bible times, fashion was determined by the hot, dry climate. Whether you were a peasant farmer or royalty, long flowing robes kept you cool. The only difference in the clothing of wealthier people was the texture and color of the material.

A person's clothes often indicated their occupation; for example, priests wore special gowns and rabbis wore blue-fringed robes. The unusual clothes of religious leaders distinguished them from common folk and signified their authority in the community.

DON'T LEAVE HOME WITHOUT IT

Both men and women wore a tunic that they covered with a long wool garment called a cloak. Most people owned only one because they were expensive due to the difficulty and time involved in making them. Usually a person's cloak was one of their most valuable and versatile possessions. This all-purpose coat was used as a blanket to sit on, as a carry-all bag, as bedding on cool nights, even as a pledge for a debt. It was so important to people that the law required the return of a person's cloak before nightfall (Exodus 22:26).

Typical Outfits

BEST-DRESSED MEN

The elements of a typical male wardrobe included. . .

An inner tunic: like an undershirt usually made of cotton or linen. Worn in cooler weather. Varied from thigh-length to ankle-length.

The tunic-coat: a close-fitting, shirtlike garment. The most frequently worn garment at home and out on the town. Most often long-sleeved, floor-length, and solid colored. Working men or slaves sometimes wore knee length, without sleeves. Very important men wore all white.

The girdle: a cloth or leather belt worn over the tunic-coat. When the cloth girdle was drawn around the waist and tied in the back, it functioned like a belly pack carrying snacks or loose change. The leather girdle was two to six inches wide. Could have been studded with iron, silver, or gold. Worn by men who lived in the desert, tended cattle, or lived a rough life. With a shoulder strap they often held a knife or a wallet.

The cloak, mantle, or robe: a large, loose-fitting garment worn over everything else. For the working man it was made of wool, goat hair, or camel hair. For the man of distinction it was made of linen, wool, velvet, or silk, and could be elaborately bordered and lined with fur.

The headdress: three varieties: the cap (brimless cotton or wool), the turban (thick linen scarf or sash wound around the head concealing the ends), and the headscarf (square yard of cotton, wool, or silk draped around the head and held in place by several silk twists.

The shoes or sandals: shoes were of soft leather (moccasin-like); sandals were made of a rougher, more durable leather.

Accessories: nose rings, rings.

FASHION STATEMENTS

Even in the days of the Bible, there were people who were remembered for what they wore or for their general glamour quotient. Just to mention a few. . .

John the Baptist was noted for his camel's hair clothing accessorized with a leather belt (Matthew 3:4).

Jeremiah wore custom jewelry by fashioning a necklace into the shape of an ox's yoke (Jeremiah 27).

Absalom was remembered for his thick and long hair, even in his death (2 Samuel 14:25–26).

The Ishmaelites were a whole tribe known for their gold earrings (Judges 8:24).

You might remember Samson. His long hair was braided into seven braids (Judges 16:19).

Joseph, one of Jacob's twelve sons, was renowned for his richly ornamented robe (Genesis 37:3).

Adam and Eve were the quintessence of understatement in their garments of skins made by God Himself (Genesis 3:21).

No one could forget Solomon's lovely bride, with strings of jewels and earrings of gold studded with silver (Song of Solomon 1:10–11).

Jezebel dressed for her own execution in gaudy eye makeup and a new hairdo (2 Kings 9:30–31).

Even the priests were known to wear tunics and turbans of only fine linen (Exodus 28:4).

As a child, the prophet Samuel could be seen each year in a new robe (1 Samuel 2:19).

BEST-DRESSED WOMEN

Women's clothes were similar in item to men's, but purposefully made to look feminine through embroidery and needlework.

Tunic: reaching to the feet often with fringe at the bottom with a girdle of silk or wool

Headdress: made with a very different cloth than a man's head covering. Often it was a thin veil fastened over a stiff kind of cap set with spangle ornaments.

Undergarments: cotton, linen, or silk, as would fit her station in life

Gown: often floor-length with pointed sleeves

Petticoat: a small jacket sporting fine needlework

Accessories: earrings (also called chains, pendants), nose rings, anklets (spangles), bracelets, elaborately braided hair

Social Structure in Bible Times

BREAKING THE MOLD

In Bible times, men were trained for farming, hunting, and fighting in wars. Women typically tended the children and cared for the needs of the home. Women had few rights; for example, they were not considered reliable witnesses in legal matters. Occasionally the Bible tells of women stepping out of their traditional roles to serve as judge (Deborah, Judges 4:4), worship leader (Miriam, Exodus 15:20), and prophet (Huldah, 2 Kings 22:14–20).

A SERVANT'S WORLD

The quality of a slave's life depended almost entirely on the nationality and character of his master. Roman law decreed that slaves were the legal property of their master, giving Roman masters complete control and authority over their servants. Jewish law provided slaves with limited rights, although they were still expected to obey their masters. Scripture required Jewish people to grant their Hebrew slaves freedom in the seventh year and a special year of celebration known as the Jubilee Year (Leviticus 25:39–42; Deuteronomy 15:12).

Most slaves were forced to do manual labor, but some were nurses, tutors, and even doctors. In fact, some educated people would sell themselves into slavery for a limited period of time to acquire Roman citizenship.

CHRIST'S SOCIAL REVOLUTION

Christ and the early church broke the social rules of His day. He gave honor and rights to groups that were not very high on the social ladder.

He recognized women as important: Women were among His followers, and special mention is made of them in the Gospels. The book of 1 Timothy speaks of deaconesses, and 1 Corinthians protects their marital rights.

Servants were protected: The apostle Paul urged his friend to treat his slave with respect, honor, and love (Philemon).

Social walls were destroyed: In Christ, no group of people is better than any other group. "There is neither Jew nor Gentile, neither slave nor free, nor is there male and female, for you are all one in Christ Jesus" (Galatians 3:28).

MORE THAN A MISTRESS

Concubines were common in ancient times, even among the Israelites. A concubine was considered a wife but had fewer legal rights. A few Bible passages give glimpses of the mental anguish and strife that existed in families when wives and concubines competed for the husband's affection.

The story of Sarah and Hagar in Genesis 16 is one powerful example. Sarah gave her Egyptian slave, Hagar, to her husband, Abraham, to bear children for her. In that day, giving substitute wives for childbearing was a common practice, even a requirement. After Hagar served as a surrogate mother and bore Abraham a son, Sarah mistreated and abused her because she was jealous of her ability to conceive.

Some kings in ancient times had so many concubines that they would build a separate building for them near the palace called a harem. The harem was filled with young virgins taken from their homes for one reason—to serve the king and fulfill his sexual needs. Some of these women lived in the harem all of their lives, only to be summoned by the king once. In the book of Esther, you'll read the story of a young Jewish girl who became part of the harem of a Persian king named Xerxes. The king was so pleased with Esther that he crowned her queen. Even though a queen held more influence than a concubine, she enjoyed limited rights because she lived in a male-dominated society.

Solomon was another Jew who was lured into polygamy. He married hundreds of wives to build political alliances with surrounding nations. However, the pagan practices and idolatry of his wives led to his downfall.

MORTAL ENEMIES

In the ancient world, mutual hatred and intense rivalries existed between certain groups of people, resulting in countless invasions, sieges, and wars. Longtime enemies of Israel included the Philistines, Assyrians, Ammonites, and Egyptians. One story illustrates the level to which discrimination and racial prejudice were ingrained in the culture. In Genesis 37 you'll discover the story of Joseph, who was sold into slavery in Egypt. God protected him and miraculously paved the way for him to be promoted to "second-in-command" by the Pharaoh. But despite his rank, he was forced to eat his meals apart from his Egyptian subordinates. Egyptians considered a Hebrew shepherd, like Joseph, far below them and refused to share a meal with him.

In the New Testament, you'll read about the hatred Jewish people had for Samaritans. When the Assyrians invaded the northern kingdom of Israel in 722 B.C., they deported many foreigners to settle there. Over time, the Jewish people and Assyrians intermarried, creating a mixed race called the Samaritans. "Pure-bred" Jewish people from the southern kingdom refused to associate with Samaritans because they considered them "half-breeds."

ROLES IN THE EARLY CHURCH

Teachers, deacons, elders, preachers, evangelists, missionaries, and administrators. Many important roles were filled by both men and women in the early church. The qualifications for church leaders included

- a strong faith in God and the infilling of the Holy Spirit,
- a morally upright lifestyle,
- an eagerness to serve,
- a greater concern for what they could give than what they could get,
- an understanding of the importance of caring for God's people, and an ability to lead others through godly example.

Leaders in the early church were commissioned for ministry through an ancient Jewish practice, laying on of hands. Praying and laying hands on someone set them apart for ministry and special service (Numbers 27:23; Deuteronomy 34:9; Acts 6:6).

The Job Market in Bible Times

EMPLOYMENT OPPORTUNITIES

"What do you want to be when you grow up?" Hebrew boys probably dreamed of embarking on exotic adventures when they grew up. But most often, they followed in their father's footsteps, either inheriting farmland or working in the business handed down through the family.

Israel was an agricultural community, so most work tended to relate to farming or a village craft. This list of job descriptions will give you a glimpse into the job scene in the Middle East during Bible times.

Farmers

Most peasant families supported themselves through farming. After the fall rains, when the soil was soft, farmers used wooden plows to prepare the dirt for planting. Seeds were hand scattered, after which farmers depended on steady spring rains to bring the crops. They harvested by pulling out whole plants by hand or by using a wooden sickle to cut the grain stalks. The husks were separated from the grain on the threshing floor, a hard, smooth area outside of the house. A large, forked tool was used in the winnowing process to toss the grain into the air, allowing the evening wind to blow away the chaff. The quality grain left was measured and prepared for meals in the home or for sale in the village market.

Fishermen

During Old Testament times, the Israelites did not depend heavily on fishing. But by the time of the New Testament, we discover that there was a flourishing fishing industry around the Sea of Galilee. Fish were so abundant that some fishermen stood on the shores, threw out a circle of netting (weighted around the edges), and pulled in a good catch of fish. Most fishermen, however, used boats to take them farther out into the lake. Often, a net with weights on the bottom and corks on the top would be thrown out between two fishing boats and dragged to shore.

Bible stories tell us most about the fishing business during this time. One recorded interaction between Jesus and His disciples reveals that some fishermen worked all night at their job (John 21:3–4). A career in fishing could be dangerous because of the prevalence of unpredictable storms on the Sea of Galilee. One such event is recorded in Matthew 8:23–27.

Artisans

Some Jewish people supported their families by producing crafts and artifacts to sell. Potters made clay cooking and eating utensils. Carpenters made plows, winnowing forks, and threshing tools for farming, as well as simple furniture for homes. Tanners fashioned cowhide and goatskin into sandals, bags, and water sacks. Masons molded and shaped limestone rocks to be used in construction.

Shepherds

Shepherds usually were responsible for a flock of sheep and goats mixed together. Their tasks included feeding the flock, leading it to green pastures, protecting the animals from wild animals, and keeping track of the flock. Shepherds sometimes had to travel far with their herds to find pastures, especially in the hot summer months.

Both goats and sheep were valuable: goats for milk, meat, and their hair, which was used to make clothing, and sheep for their wool and meat.

THE *JERUSALEM GAZETTE* CLASSIFIED SECTION

Assistant Manager: Local innkeeper is looking for an assistant manager to train for the night shift. Responsibilities include recording reservations, greeting patrons, occasional deliveries, supervising support staff, light cleaning duties, and quality control. Strong communication skills a must. Experience in innkeeping and management is preferred. We offer a modest salary with great benefits (free meals and housing).

Sales Representative: Jerusalem Farming Products is a leader in the manufacture and distribution of quality farming products and equipment. We have an opportunity available to promote the sale of our products within a new neighboring territory. The individual we seek will develop and maintain a distribution network while managing distribution sales and marketing. Knowledge of farming tools is required. Only qualified applicants need apply.

Horse-Drawn Cart Driver: Experienced cart driver needed. Must have good attitude, dress well, have impeccable driving record, and possess good knowledge of Jerusalem and surrounding areas. For salary and benefits information, see Jotham, son of Abijah.

Apprentice Carpenter: Busy carpentry shop looking for eager and diligent apprentice. No experience required but good references a must. Hours include evenings and alternate Saturdays. Walk-ins welcome at Azor's Carpentry Corner.

Priests

The office of priest was established by God to mediate between God and the nation of Israel. Priests were Levites descended from Aaron, Israel's first high priest. They were responsible for helping the common people maintain a right relationship with God, as well as overseeing the everyday operations of the temple and maintaining the system of daily sacrifices on behalf of the people.

Levites (they were descendants of Levi, not Aaron) had different jobs than priests in the temple. Although they did not have the authority and responsibilities of the priests, they were very important to the smooth operation and upkeep of the temple.

Places in Bible Times

HOME SWEET HOME

In ancient times, Middle Eastern homes were built of mud bricks, usually on a stone or limestone foundation. Outside staircases led to flat roofs that provided a sitting area and extra storage space. Small windows allowed air flow but kept out intruders. Most houses had a small raised area for sleeping. Only wealthier people had upper rooms, courtyards, or gardens.

TABERNACLES, TEMPLES, AND SYNAGOGUES

Why are these different terms used in the Bible? The tabernacle, temple, and synagogue were all places of worship for the Israelites, but they also had distinct differences.

Before God's people reached the Promised Land, they wandered in the desert for many years. Because of their nomadic lifestyle, they needed a portable place of worship. A tent, also called the tabernacle, served the purpose well.

After the Israelites had settled in the Promised Land and enjoyed peace from the wars it took to conquer the land, King Solomon built the temple, a permanent place for the people to worship God and offer sacrifices. The ark of the Lord's covenant was placed in the temple to symbolize God's presence there.

In the New Testament, local synagogues were built to provide local places of worship. These synagogues and the temple itself became the main places of worship. Devout Jewish people visited the temple whenever possible, but between visits, they worshipped in their local synagogues. While the women and children waited in a gallery, the men participated in religious services.

THE ORDER OF SERVICE

Synagogue services were much like Christian church services today. Services usually included

- a creed,
- prayers,
- selections read aloud from the Law and the Prophets,
- a sermon, and
- a time of questions and answers.

SCHOOL AT CHURCH

The courts of the temple in Jerusalem became places of education, especially during the time of Passover when the greatest religious teachers would gather to teach and debate theological issues among themselves.

Two biblical examples refer to these temple courts, which were known throughout the land to be great places of learning. First, Mary and Joseph found their young son, Jesus, in the temple courts discussing the deepest spiritual truths and toughest questions with the religious leaders and teachers of the law (Luke 2:41–49). Second, we know the apostle Paul was educated in Jerusalem, probably in the temple courts, under one of the most honored rabbis of the first century, Gamaliel (Acts 22:3).

WHERE'S THE "MOOLAH"?

One poignant story in the New Testament (found in Luke 21:1–4) introduces us to another interesting place—the temple treasury. A poor widow caught the attention of Jesus when she gave all the money she had as a freewill offering to the Lord.

Located either in the court of women or in an adjacent walkway, the treasury was the place where people deposited their tithes and offerings. Seven boxes were designated for the temple tax and six were for freewill offerings.

LIFE IN THE "BIG HOUSE"

In Bible times, criminals endured vile conditions in prisons. Prisoners like Joseph (Genesis 39:20) were considered guilty until proven innocent and forced to do hard labor until their trial or until they died, whichever came first.

Often prisoners were stripped, beaten with a whip, and put into stocks in the jail. Stocks were two boards connected with iron clamps that held in place a person's wrists and ankles. For the gory details, read the story of Paul and Silas in Acts 16:22–23.

4

BIBLES AND
TRANSLATIONS

Which Bible Is the Best?

Want to be overwhelmed? Go stand in front of the Bible display at your local Christian bookstore and ask yourself the question, "Which Bible is best for me?"

There's no easy answer. And if you stand in front of that Bible display long enough, you'll start to wonder if there's an answer at all. Take heart; there is. That big display is actually pretty well organized, and you have a lot of good options to choose from. In short, it's not as bad as you think. But there are three questions you need to answer in order to navigate your Bible bookstore.

WHICH TRANSLATION WOULD YOU LIKE?

There are many good translations to choose from. While there is no best translation, there are certain translations that are better for certain kinds of studying. To get a little more specific, we've got to get a little technical, so grab a cup of coffee and hang with us for two minutes.

The Bible was originally written in Greek, Hebrew, and Aramaic. There are two ways to translate these languages, just like there are two ways to translate any other language (like French or Spanish).

Word for Word

This translation philosophy looks at each individual word and translates it into the English equivalent. These translations can be a little tougher to read and use big, theological words.

Thought for Thought

This translation philosophy looks at phrases, not individual words. Rather than translate each word one at a time, the translator looks at the whole phrase or sentence and asks: "How can I translate this thought into an English phrase that means the same thing?" These translations are easier to read.

Which method is better? Neither. Word-for-word translations (like the KJV or the NASB) are very helpful in studying a single verse or doing word studies. But a thought-for-thought translation (like the NIV or NLT) is very good for daily reading. Some linguists call word-for-word translations "study translations" and thought-for-thought translations "reading translations." We recommend that you have at least one of each on your bookshelf.

The spectrum below shows you where the bestselling Bible translations fall between the two translation philosophies:

KJV	**NASB**	**NKJV**	**NRSV**	**NIV**	**NLT**	**NCV**	**CEV**	**NIrV**

Word for Word   *Thought for Thought*
Study Translations   *Reading Translations*

WOULD YOU LIKE STUDY HELPS WITH YOUR BIBLE?

You can buy a plain Bible, or you can buy a Bible with lots of extra stuff to help you understand and apply the Bible. For example, you can buy a Bible with maps that show you where different cities are. Or you can buy a Bible that has a concordance in the back for those times you want to look up a verse but don't remember where it is. It's like combining a Bible encyclopedia with your Bible. While these features aren't the inspired Word of God, they help you better understand and navigate the Bible.

There are other features you can choose from, too. *Study Bibles* give you background, historical data, and explanations of hard-to-understand verses. *Devotional Bibles* give you a devotional plan for reading the Bible each day. They give you a daily Bible verse to read and give you a devotional thought (kind of like a short sermon) on the passage. You have a lot of options in this category, so you can pick one that has themes you would like to study regularly. For example, you might want to help revive your spiritual life and might choose the *Praise and Worship Bible* (Tyndale) or the *Bible for Personal Revival* (Zondervan). You might decide you need help applying the Bible and choose the *Life Application Bible*. There are many good options for you that will help you read the Bible regularly.

If you buy a Bible with study helps, you need to remember that those helps (while very useful) are not the Bible. God's Word is what the original writers wrote between Genesis and Revelation. Any commentary is just someone's interpretation.

WOULD YOU LIKE THAT IN SOFTCOVER, HARDCOVER, OR LEATHER?

Most Bibles can be delivered in a number of binding options. Softcover Bibles are inexpensive, but not as durable. They're great for giving away or for reference, but they're not very practical for everyday use because they'll tear or wear out. Hardcover Bibles are durable and will serve you well. Leather Bibles are best made and can help you distinguish your Bible from other books. Many people like leather Bibles because the leather reminds them that this book is extra special. Keep in mind that there are differing grades of leather (the nicer the leather, the more expensive).

5

WHERE TO FIND IT

Where to Find It

Many editions of the Bible include a concordance in the back. This is like an index. Names, places, events, and words are listed there with their correlating scripture reference. There are also larger, comprehensive concordances you can buy to accompany your Bible.

Included below is a short concordance of easily recognized people, events, and well-known passages.

Abraham almost sacrifices Isaac . . . . Genesis 22:1–18

Adam and Eve: the first man and woman . . Genesis 2:1–3:24

Balaam and the talking donkey . . . . Numbers 22:21–36

Beatitudes: Jesus' Sermon on the Mount . . . Matthew 5:1–12

Cain kills Abel: the first murder . . . . Genesis 4

Creation. . . . . Genesis 1:1–2:3

Daniel in the lions' den . . . . Daniel 6:1–23

Daniel's friends in the fiery furnace. . . . . . . Daniel 3:1–30

David is anointed king. . . . . 1 Samuel 16:7–13

Elijah faces Baal's prophets on Mt. Carmel. . . 1 Kings 18:16–40

Elijah's chariot of fire. . . . . 2 Kings 2:9–15

Esau, Isaac's son, sells his birthright . . . . . . Genesis 25:27–34

Faith chapter (aka the Hall of Faith). . . . . . Hebrews 11

First Passover in Egypt . . . . Exodus 12:1–30

First sin . . . . Genesis 3:1–24

Fruit of the Spirit . . . . Galatians 5:22–23

Garden of Eden. . . . . Genesis 2:4–3:24

Golden rule . . . . Matthew 7:12

Great commission . . . . Matthew 28:18–20

Handwriting on the wall . . . . Daniel 5:5–28

Holy Spirit comes at Pentecost . . . . Acts 2:1–13

Jericho's walls fall down . . . . Joshua 6:1–27

Jesus is baptized. . . . . Matthew 3:13–17

Jesus is born	Luke 2:1–20
Jesus is crucified	Matthew 27:33–50
Jesus is resurrected	Mark 16:1–12
Jesus is tempted	Matthew 4:1–11
Jesus is the Bread of Life	John 6:35
Jesus is the Gate	John 10:7
Jesus is the Good Shepherd	John 10:11
Jesus is the Light of the World	John 8:12
Jesus is the Vine	John 15:1
Jesus is the Way, the Truth, and the Life	John 14:6
Jesus is transfigured	Luke 9:28–36
Jesus walks on water	Matthew 14:22–52
John the Baptist is killed	Mark 6:14–29
John the Baptist's ministry	Matthew 3:1–6
Jonah and the big fish	Jonah 1:1–2:10
Jordan River is parted by God	Joshua 3:1–17
Joseph is taken to Egypt	Genesis 37:1–36
King David and Bathsheba	2 Samuel 11:1–27
King David and Goliath	1 Samuel 17:1–58
Lazarus is raised from the dead	John 11:1–44
Lord's Prayer	Matthew 6:9–13
Lot's wife turns to salt	Genesis 19:15–26
Love chapter (a famous wedding reading)	1 Corinthians 13
Moses and the burning bush	Exodus 3:1–22
Moses and the golden calf	Exodus 32:1–35
Moses leads the Hebrews out of Egypt	Exodus 12:31–14:31
Moses protected as a baby	Exodus 2:1–10
Naaman is healed of leprosy	2 Kings 5:1–19
Nicodemus talks with Jesus	John 3:1–21
Noah and the flood	Genesis 6:9–8:22
Noah and the ark	Genesis 6:1–9:17
Paul and Silas sing in prison	Acts 16:16–40

Paul's conversion . . . . Acts 9:1–19
Paul's shipwreck. . . . . Acts 27:13–28:10
Peter's escape from prison . . . . Acts 12:1–19
Plagues on Egypt. . . . . Exodus 7–11
Rainbow after the flood. . . . . Genesis 9:8–17
Red Sea is parted by God . . . . Exodus 14:5–31
Samson and Delilah . . . . Judges 16:4–22
Sermon on the Mount. . . . . Matthew 5–7
Sodom and Gomorrah. . . . . Genesis 19:1–28
Stephen is stoned. . . . . Acts 7:54–60
Sun stands still. . . . . Joshua 10:1–15
Ten Commandments. . . . . Exodus 20:1–17
Tower of Babel: languages are created . . . . . Genesis 11:1–9
Wise men visit Jesus . . . . Matthew 2:1–12
Zacchaeus meets Jesus. . . . . Luke 19:1–10

Who's Who?

Aaron: Moses' brother, the first high priest . . . Exodus 4
Abel: Adam and Eve's second son . . . . Genesis 4
Abraham: Father of the Jewish nation . . . . . Genesis 18
Adam: The first man God created . . . . Genesis 2
Barnabas: Paul's early missionary
    companion. . . . . Acts 13
Bathsheba: The woman with whom King
    David had an affair . . . . 2 Samuel 11
Boaz: The husband of Ruth . . . . Ruth 2
Cain: Adam and Eve's first son . . . . Genesis 4
Daniel: A young Israelite who became a
    leader in Persia. Also survived the lions.. . Daniel 1
David: A shepherd, a musician, and the
    second king of Israel . . . . 1 Samuel 17

Deborah: The only female leader (judge)
of the Hebrews that we know of . . . . . . Judges 4

Delilah: Woman who tricked Samson into
cutting his hair . . . . Judges 16

Disciples: The followers of Jesus, but usually
it means the twelve he was closest to:
Simon Peter, Andrew, James, John,
Philip, Bartholomew, Thomas, Matthew,
James the son of Alphaeus, Thaddaeus,
Simon the Zealot, Judas Iscariot . . . . . . Matthew 10

Elijah: A great prophet . . . . 1 Kings 17

Elisha: A great prophet who learned
under Elijah . . . . 1 Kings 19

Esau: One of Isaac and Rebekah's twins,
later named Edom. . . . . Genesis 25

Esther: Jewish beauty who became queen
of Persia. . . . . Esther 2

Eve: The first woman God created. . . . . . . Genesis 2

Gideon: A judge or leader of the Hebrews
who put a fleece before God . . . . Judges 6

Hannah: Samuel's mother . . . . 1 Samuel 1

Herod: The king who feared Jesus' birth
so ordered all baby boys killed. . . . . Matthew 2

Isaac: Abraham's son . . . . Genesis 20, 22

Jacob: One of Isaac and Rebekah's twins,
later named Israel . . . . Genesis 25

Jesus: Son of God, Savior of the world . . . . . Luke 2

Jochebed: Moses' mother . . . . Exodus 1–2

John the Baptist: Jesus' cousin. John
introduced Jesus to the world . . . . Matthew 3

Jonathan: Saul's son and David's best friend . . 1 Samuel 18–20

Joseph: Favorite son of Jacob who established
    leadership in Egypt . . . . Genesis 37

Joshua: Leader of the Hebrews
    after Moses . . . . Numbers 13–14

Judas Iscariot: The disciple who
    betrayed Christ. . . . . Matthew 26–27

Lazarus: Friend of Jesus,
    brother of Mary and Martha. . . . . John 11

Leah: Jacob's wife. . . . . Genesis 29

Levites: Descendants of Levi whose tribe
    was assigned to assist priests . . . . Numbers 1

Lot: Abraham's nephew who lived in
    Sodom and Gomorrah . . . . Genesis 13, 19

Mary: Mother of Jesus. . . . . Matthew 2

Mary and Martha: Friends of Jesus,
    sisters of Lazarus. . . . . Luke 10

Miriam: Moses' sister. . . . . Exodus 2; Numbers 12

Mordecai: Esther's cousin who was
    like a father to her. . . . . Esther 2

Moses: Leader of the Hebrews when
    they exited Egypt . . . . Exodus 2

Naomi: A Jewish woman who lost her
    husband and sons in Moab and
    traveled back to Bethlehem with her
    daughter-in-law Ruth . . . . Ruth 1

Noah: The only faithful man on the earth
    before the flood. . . . . Genesis 5–6

Paul: The apostle, a persecutor of the
    church converted to a missionary . . . . . Acts 8–9

Pilate: The governor who tried Jesus
    but could not find Him guilty. . . . . Matthew 27

Priscilla and Aquila: Friends of Paul
the apostle. . . . . Acts 18

Prophets: Preachers in the Old and
New Testaments who called the
people of God back to obedience
and sometimes spoke of the future . . . . *various books*

Rachel: Jacob's favorite wife . . . . Genesis 29

Rahab: A prostitute in Jericho who
helped the Jewish spies and so saved
her life and the life of her family . . . . . . Joshua 2, 6

Rebekah: Isaac's wife. . . . . Genesis 24

Ruth: Naomi's daughter-in-law who
traveled with Naomi back
to Bethlehem. . . . . Ruth 1

Samson: A judge whose long hair and
Nazirite code gave him superhuman
strength. . . . . Judges 13–14

Sarah: Abraham's wife . . . . Genesis 11, 17

Saul: The first king of Israel. . . . . 1 Samuel 9

Seth: Adam and Eve's third son . . . . Genesis 4

Shadrach, Meshach, and Abednego:
Friends of Daniel taken captive
in Persia. . . . . Daniel 1, 3

Silas: Paul's later missionary companion . . . Acts 15

Stephen: The first Christian martyr . . . . Acts 6–7

Solomon: Third and wisest king of Israel,
David and Bathsheba's son . . . . 1 Kings 2

Timothy: Apprentice of the apostle Paul . . . 1 Timothy 1

Zacchaeus: Short tax collector who saw
Jesus by climbing a tree. . . . . Luke 19

Women Who Made a Difference

Abigail	1 Samuel 25:1–42; 2 Samuel 3:3
Anna	Luke 2:36–38
Deborah	Judges 4–5
Dorcas	Acts 9:36–42
Elizabeth	Luke 1:5–80
Esther	The book of Esther
Eunice	Acts 16:1–3; 2 Timothy 1:5
Eve	Genesis 2–3; 2 Corinthians 11:3; 1 Timothy 2:13
Hannah	1 Samuel 1; 2:1–21
Jochebed	Exodus 2:1–11; 6:20; Numbers 26:59
Lois	2 Timothy 1:5
Lydia	Acts 16:12–15, 40
Martha	Luke 10:38–41; John 11; 12:1–3
Mary Magdalene	Matthew 27:56, 61; 28:1; John 19:25; 20:1–18
Mary, mother of Jesus	Matthew 1–2; 12:46; Luke 1–2; John 2:1–11; 19:25; Acts 1:14
Miriam	Exodus 15:20–21; Numbers 12:1–15; 20:1; 26:59
Naomi	The book of Ruth
Phoebe	Romans 16:1–2
Priscilla	Acts 18:2, 18, 26; Romans 16:3
Rachel	Genesis 29–31; 33:1–2, 7
Rahab	Joshua 2:1, 3; 6:17–25; Hebrews 11:31

The Parables of Jesus

Jesus often taught by telling stories called parables. Parables are stories that may or may not have been true but always have a spiritual interpretation. Sometimes Jesus interpreted His parables for the people and sometimes He left them to interpret them.

The parables listed here are in the order in which they appear in the Gospels.

The Sower, the Seed, the Soils: A story about seed sown on different types of soils. These soils reflect our own hearts and the way we accept God's truth (Matthew 13:3–8; Mark 4:2–8; Luke 8:4–8).

The Weeds and the Wheat: An enemy of a farmer sows weeds into his wheat field. Alludes to the final judgment when God identifies those of true faith (Matthew 13:24–30).

The Mustard Seed: Something so small as a seed can grow to be a large plant or tree. Faith works like this. A small amount goes a long way (Matthew 13:31–32; Mark 4:30–32; Luke 13:18–19).

The Yeast: The kingdom of God is like yeast that, even in small amounts, changes the shape of a whole loaf of bread (Matthew 13:33; Luke 13:20–21).

The Treasure: The kingdom of God is like a treasure (Matthew 13:44).

The Pearl: The kingdom of God is like a precious pearl. It is more valuable than everything else (Matthew 13:45–46).

The Good and Bad Fish: Alludes to the judgment when evil people are separated from good people (Matthew 13:47–50).

The Lost Sheep: A shepherd's commitment to one sheep mirrors God's commitment to each of us (Matthew 18:12–14; Luke 15:3–7).

The Unforgiving Servant: A man who has had a great debt canceled won't cancel a small debt owed to him. Speaks to unforgiveness (Matthew 18:23–35).

The Workers on Payday: Explains the kingdom of heaven in terms of workers who are paid the same wage, no matter when they signed on (Matthew 20:1–16).

The Two Sons: One son says no but then does as he is told. The other says yes but never gets the job done (Matthew 21:28–32).

The Vineyard: A man leaves some sharecroppers in charge of his vineyard. When they don't care for it, he finds others to take their place. Speaks to our accountability before God (Matthew 21:33–46; Mark 12:1–9; Luke 20:9–16).

The Marriage Feast: Many are invited to a feast, but not many come. Speaks to our invitation into the kingdom of God (Matthew 22:1–14).

The Foolish Manager: A manager ignores his superior's instructions and is caught red-handed. Speaks to our accountability at the final judgment (Matthew 24:45–51; Luke 12:42–48).

The Bridesmaids: According to an old custom the bridesmaids wait for the groom, but some are unprepared. Speaks to our final accountability before God (Matthew 25:1–13).

The Three Investors: The boss goes away, leaving money to be invested. Only those who invest wisely are rewarded (Matthew 25:14–30; Luke 19:11–27).

The Wheat Harvest: The kingdom of God is like a seed that by its own magic grows into a harvest (Mark 4:26–29).

The Watchful Servant: A man leaves a servant in charge of his house but doesn't give the time of his return. That servant must always keep watch. Speaks to Christ's second coming (Mark 13:34–37).

The Canceled Loans: Two loans are canceled. One is large, one is small. Which debtor will be the most grateful? Speaks to God's forgiveness (Luke 7:40–43).

The Good Samaritan: A man who is undesirable himself is the true neighbor because he cares for someone (Luke 10:30–37).

The Request at Midnight: Insight on prayer. A friend makes a request at an inconvenient time but gets what he wants if he keeps on asking (Luke 11:5–10).

The Rich Fool: A rich man keeps storing more and getting more, but when he dies he loses it all (Luke 12:16–21).

The Fruitless Fig Tree: A tree that is supposed to produce fruit doesn't and is given one more year (Luke 13:6–9).

The Best Seat: Don't pick the best seat at a feast or you might be embarrassed. Pick the worst seat and let the host move you to the head table (Luke 14:7–11).

The Banquet Invitations: A man invites many to his banquet, but when they don't come he invites everyone he can find. Speaks to the kingdom of God (Luke 14:15–24).

The Lost Coin: A woman's search for a lost coin mirrors God's commitment to people (Luke 15:8–10).

The Prodigal Son: A son's journey away from family and home and his subsequent return mirror our journey through life and God's ever-welcoming arms (Luke 15:11–32).

The Shrewd Businessman: A dishonest manager in danger of losing his job makes a few friends on his way down (Luke 16:1–10).

The Servant's Duty: A servant shouldn't expect to be thanked for doing his duty (Luke 17:7–10).

The Unjust Judge: Insight on prayer. A widow receives from an unjust judge because of her persistence (Luke 18:1–8).

The Pharisee and the Tax Collector Pray: The Pharisee prays out of his
pride. The tax collector prays out of his humility. The tax collector is
justified in God's eyes (Luke 18:9–14).

Miracles of Jesus

This is a list of the miracles that Jesus performed while He lived on earth as both
God and man. They are in the order they appear in the Gospels. In the places
where several Gospels record the same miracle, we've listed them together.

MIRACLES OF HEALING

- Jesus heals a man with leprosy (Matthew 8:1–4; Mark 1:40–42; Luke
  5:12–13).
- Jesus heals a soldier's servant (Matthew 8:5–13; Luke 7:1–10).
- Jesus heals Peter's mother-in-law (Matthew 8:14–15; Mark 1:29–31;
  Luke 4:38–39).
- Jesus heals a paralyzed man (Matthew 9:1–8; Mark 2:1–12; Luke
  5:17–26).
- A woman is healed by touching Jesus' clothes (Matthew 9:20–22; Mark
  5:25–34; Luke 8:43–48).
- Jesus heals a man's withered hand (Matthew 12:9–13; Mark 3:1–5; Luke
  6:6–10).
- Jesus heals the blind (Matthew 9:27–31; 20:29–34; Mark 8:22–25;
  10:46–52; Luke 18:35–43; John 9:1–7).
- Jesus heals a man who cannot see or hear (Mark 7:31–37).
- Jesus heals a crippled woman (Luke 13:10–13).
- Jesus cures a sick man (Luke 14:1–4).
- Jesus heals ten lepers (Luke 17:11–19).
- Jesus reattaches a man's ear (Luke 22:49–51).
- Jesus heals an official's son without even meeting him (John 4:46–54).
- Jesus heals a man who had been an invalid for thirty-eight years (John
  5:1–16).

MIRACLES OF PROVISION

- Jesus feeds five thousand men plus women and children from five loaves and two fish (Matthew 14:15–21; Mark 6:35–44; Luke 9:12–17; John 6:5–14).
- Jesus feeds four thousand men plus women and children from seven loaves and a few fish (Matthew 15:32–38; Mark 8:1–9).
- The disciples catch a miraculous netful of fish (Luke 5:1–7).
- Jesus turns water into wine (John 2:1–11).
- Jesus brings in another miraculous catch of fish after His resurrection (John 21:1–14).

MIRACLES THAT INVOLVED RAISING SOMEONE FROM THE DEAD

- Jesus raises Jairus's daughter from the dead (Matthew 9:18–26; Mark 5:22–24, 35–43; Luke 8:41–42, 49–56).
- A widow's son is raised from the dead (Luke 7:11–16).
- Lazarus is raised from the dead (John 11:1–45).

MIRACLES THAT INVOLVED CASTING OUT DEMONS

- Jesus casts demons out of a man and sends them into pigs (Matthew 8:28–34; Mark 5:1–19; Luke 8:26–39).
- Jesus casts out a demon and a mute man can speak (Matthew 9:32–33; 12:22; Luke 11:14).
- Jesus casts a demon out of the daughter of a foreigner (Matthew 15:21–28; Mark 7:24–30).
- Jesus heals a boy possessed by a demon (Matthew 17:14–18; Mark 9:14–26; Luke 9:37–42).
- Jesus casts out a demon at the synagogue (Mark 1:23–27; Luke 4:33–36).

OTHER MIRACLES

- Jesus stills the storm with His voice (Matthew 8:23–27; Mark 4:36–40; Luke 8:22–24).
- Jesus walks on top of rough waters (Matthew 14:22–33; Mark 6:45–52; John 6:17–21).
- Jesus curses a fig tree (Matthew 21:18–22; Mark 11:12–14, 20–22).

FINDING HELP WHEN YOU NEED IT

When you're...

tired. . . . . Psalm 23
hurting . . . . Hebrews 12
tempted . . . . Daniel 1; 1 Corinthians 10; James 1
needing some courage . . . . Joshua 1; Ephesians 6
needing some good advice . . . . Proverbs
depressed. . . . . Psalm 42
struggling with right and wrong. . . . . Matthew 5–7; Colossians 2
wondering who Jesus is . . . . John 6–10
trying to figure out the Church. . . . . 1 Corinthians 12
feeling offended by someone . . . . 1 Corinthians 6
finding it hard to believe . . . . Hebrews 11
needing to forgive someone . . . . Philemon
discouraged . . . . Romans 8
afraid. . . . . Psalm 27
feeling like giving up . . . . 2 Timothy 2
happy . . . . Psalm 95
wishing you hadn't said something . . . . James 3
struggling to do what's right . . . . Romans 7–8
not sure you're worth anything . . . . Genesis 1; Romans 4–5
wanting to be closer to God . . . . John 3
feeling guilty. . . . . 1 John 1–2; Psalm 51
lonely, left out . . . . Psalm 25
trying to be more loving . . . . 1 Corinthians 13
looking for God's will. . . . . Philippians 2
looking for guidance . . . . Psalm 25
wondering about abortion. . . . . Psalm 139
wondering if success will make you happy . . . . Ecclesiastes
wondering how to become a Christian . . . . Romans 10

6

BOOK OVERVIEWS

Genesis

NUTS AND BOLTS

The book of Genesis lays the groundwork for all the other stories in the Bible. The places, the people, the events find their roots in this book of beginnings. There are several story lines that you can follow, but it gets a little confusing to try to follow them all at once. First of all, God establishes the world and people in general. Then, when people disregard Him (as people will do), God establishes a relationship with a certain group of people in order to build a forum for faith and a setting for His redemption. We call that certain group the Jewish nation. Genesis tells us how all that came to be.

CREATION

Genesis describes the creation of the world in very concrete terms. God spoke us and our surroundings into being. He displayed His love and creativity in the variety of plants, animals, and environments, some of which we can still see today. The world was ideal when God made it. The first people were placed in a paradise called the Garden of Eden and asked to tend that garden, to build a friendship with God, and to obey Him if He asked them specifically not to do something. You probably know how that story goes. The dad was Adam, the mom was Eve. . . .

THE FIRST DYSFUNCTIONAL FAMILY

Adam and Eve were the first earth dwellers to experience the world as innocent ADULTS. They woke up for the first time able to walk and run and love and enjoy God's creation. If you've read Genesis, you know that they did NOT obey God. They did the one thing He asked them not to do. Because of this they were forced to leave their ideal garden, and thus a life much more like ours began: sweat and labor and pain and disappointment. They lost their first two children because one brother, Cain, killed the other, Abel, out of jealousy and rage. It was not a happy time. Abel was dead and Cain was exiled. But Adam and Eve did what we do today. They picked themselves up and dusted themselves off and, with the forgiveness and guidance of almighty God, they started all over again. Their world was now less than ideal, but their God was still the same.

NOAH

We assume at this point that everyone in the world is a descendant of Adam and Eve unless God created people He hasn't told us about. As generation built upon generation, the descendants of the first family disregarded God more and more. The world became a mess. (More of a mess than it is now? Probably so.) It was such a mess that God resolved that He would scrap the project and start over. He could only find one person who was worth starting over with. That was Noah, a man with a wife and three married sons.

God told Noah to build a very big boat. Chances are, it hadn't even rained in the world yet, so building a boat was a brave thing for Noah to do. God brought the animals and, with Noah's family, they all got on board. The floods began, and everything on the earth was destroyed except the creatures on that boat.

When it was all over, Noah recommitted himself, his family, and this freshly laundered world to follow the Creator once again. We are all descendants of Noah's family.

ABRAHAM

One of Noah's descendants (more than a few generations down) was Abram (whose name was later changed to Abraham by God Himself). God established a special relationship with Abraham. He promised that Abraham would be the father of a great nation. You'll understand how great was Abraham's faith when you realize that he was very old and had never had children! Abraham's faith was also shown when he picked up and moved to the place that we know as Israel today.

Eventually Abraham and his also-old wife, Sarah, did have a child, Isaac, way past their childbearing years. Here were two people who would have had top-selling autobiographies as well as incredible tabloid marketability. But in their day and time they were just two people who (after some laughter and "are you sures?") believed God would do what He said.

If you've hung around children's church much, you may have heard the silly song "Father Abraham Had Many Sons." The song can go on forever. Abraham's descendants do, too. All from two little old people who believed.

You may have heard of Sodom and Gomorrah, some very evil cities. Abraham's nephew, Lot, lived in these cities. Abraham saved Lot from destruction just before God burned the towns to the ground.

THE ISRAELITES

Genesis is all about a family tree. You'll find genealogies galore. You'll find families leading into families, and irritating as it may be to women today, most of this is defined according to the dads. This is an ironic twist considering that the test of whether a Jewish person is actually Jewish relies on the nationality of the mother and not the father.

Anyway, once Abraham is in the picture, Genesis is about the establishing of those many descendants God had promised. Abraham's son Isaac had twin sons, Esau and Jacob. Of those two, Jacob got the birthright. In that time this meant that he rose in power and notoriety. He became the leader of the family. God changed Jacob's name to Israel (names meant a lot more back then than they do now, and there wasn't any paperwork to fill out). Thus Jacob, or Israel, became the head of the family of the Israelites (or Israelis or Hebrews or Jewish people as we know them today).

Jacob had twelve sons and one daughter. His twelve sons became the twelve tribes of Israel (get it?). They were destined to develop the land of Israel and claim their ranches. It was a mideastern "Bonanza" in the making. But a famine came across the land and changed their destiny from then until now, even to the most current of current events.

JOSEPH

Jacob's favorite sons were his two youngest sons, Joseph and Benjamin. They were the sons of Jacob's favorite wife, Rachel.

Joseph was the confident sort and his older brothers resented his dreams and aspirations, whether they came from God or not. Remember this was a barbaric time. Joseph's brothers resorted to violence in their rage at their cocky younger brother. While they were in the wilderness together, they beat up Joseph and almost decided to kill him. Instead they settled for selling him into slavery.

This slavery eventually led Joseph to Egypt. While he started out in poverty, despite jail time and false accusations, through faithfulness, perseverance, and some dream interpreting on the side, Joseph became one of the pharaoh's most trusted men.

Talk about a twist of fate. Later, when Jacob's land was filled with a fierce famine, he sent his sons to Egypt begging for food. Who do you think was the man in charge of giving out portions? None other than their long-lost brother Joseph. You can imagine the shuffling feet and wary glances. It was truly a younger sibling's opportunity for revenge.

But in the end, Joseph knew that his brothers' foolish and violent actions had, in the long run, set the stage for his family's survival in the famine.

Eventually the whole family moved to Egypt and established a long-term residence there.

KEY VERSES IN GENESIS

"In the beginning God created the heavens and the earth. Now the earth was formless and empty, darkness was over the surface of the deep, and the Spirit of God was hovering over the waters. And God said, 'Let there be light,' and there was light" (Genesis 1:1–3).

"Then God said, 'Let us make mankind in our image, in our likeness, so that they may rule over the fish in the sea and the birds in the air, over the livestock and all the wild animals, and over all the creatures that move along the ground.' So God created mankind in his own image, in the image of God he created them; male and female he created them" (Genesis 1:26–27).

"The LORD saw how great the wickedness of the human race had become on the earth, and that every inclination of the thoughts of the human heart was only evil all the time. The LORD regretted that he had made human beings on the earth, and his heart was deeply troubled. So the LORD said, 'I will wipe from the face of the earth the human race I have created—and with them the animals, the birds and the creatures that move along the ground—for I regret that I have made them.' But Noah found favor in the eyes of the LORD" (Genesis 6:5–8).

"When Abram was ninety-nine years old, the LORD appeared to him and said, 'I am God Almighty; walk before me faithfully and be blameless. Then I will make my covenant between me and you and will greatly increase your numbers.' Abram fell facedown, and God said to him, 'As for me, this is my covenant with you: You will be the father of many nations. No longer will you be called Abram; your name will be Abraham, for I have made you a father of many nations. I will make you very fruitful; I will make nations of you, and kings will come from you. I will establish my covenant as an everlasting covenant between me and you and your descendants after you for the generations to come, to be your God and the God of your descendants after you'" (Genesis 17:1–7).

AN EXPLANATION YOU MIGHT NEED

Polygamy: to have more than one spouse living at a time. The historical period Genesis describes is a time in which polygamy was accepted. Since it was a culture in which men held the power, there were multiple wives more than multiple husbands. Not only were there wives (or harems), there were also concubines (sexual partners, but not marriage partners). This is difficult to reconcile in today's world where polygamy exists but is not considered a standard way of living. There was still an element of faithfulness (at least there was marriage), and throughout history God honored monogamous husband/wife relationships (after all, He didn't create Adam and Eve and Isabel).

There are also several occasions listed in Genesis where a woman offered her servant or maid to her husband to father his children. Sarah tried it with Abraham, and brought grief in her family that continues to this day. Leah and Rachel both adopted this practice with their servants. It was so important in that culture to have sons, as many of them as possible, that practices such as this were thought of as last resorts.

! NAMES

Names meant a lot in the days of Genesis. Here are some names and their meanings:

Abram	Exalted father
Abraham	Father of a multitude
Sarai	Contentious
Sarah	Princess
Jacob	Displacer
Reuben	See! A son!
Simeon	God hears
Asher	Gladness
Judah	Praise

DOES GENESIS HAVE SIGNIFICANCE IN THE COMING OF CHRIST?

Since the Bible, in its entirety, is really about Jesus, even this beginning book lays a foundation. When Adam and Eve disregarded God's one requirement for their paradise living, there was a snake involved. We believe this snake to be a force of evil (the devil, Lucifer, prince of darkness). When God explained the consequences of Eve's, Adam's, and the snake's actions, He said to the snake: "Because you have done this, 'Cursed are you above all livestock and all wild animals! You will crawl on your belly and you will eat dust all the days of your life. And I will put enmity between you and the woman, and between your offspring and hers; he will crush your head, and you will strike his heel'" (Genesis 3:14–15). This was probably a reference to Jesus coming to conquer the powers of evil.

Also in God's promise to Abraham was the promise that the Messiah (the Savior, Jesus Christ) would come through that family line.

WHO SAID IT?

"You intended to harm me, but God intended it for good to accomplish what is now being done, the saving of many lives."
—Joseph, Israel's son who had been sold into Egypt and later saved his family's life because of it. (Genesis 50:20)

"The woman you put here with me—she gave me some fruit. . . ."
—Adam's response to God after the Fall. (Genesis 3:12)

"Will a son be born to a man a hundred years old?"
—Abraham's response to the news that he would be a dad. (Genesis 17:17)

"I regret that I have made them."
—God's response to the behavior of the world in the days of Noah. (Genesis 6:7)

Here are some phrases you might hear today that actually came from Genesis. . . .
Adam's rib (God used Adam's rib to make Eve.)
Coat of many colors (It belonged to Joseph, Israel's son.)
Am I my brother's keeper? (Cain's response after he had killed his brother.)
Jacob's ladder (Jacob had a dream about this while he was on the road.)

Exodus

VITAL STATISTICS

Name: Exodus means "a going out." (Note the similarity to "Exit.")

When written: Somewhere between 1441 and 1300 B.C. (at least 3,300 years ago)

Author: Moses

Kind of book: Narrative (story). The book of Exodus tells true stories about true events.

In a nutshell: Led by Moses, the Israelites traveled from slavery in Egypt to the border of the land promised to their ancestors.

Names you might recognize: Moses, Pharaoh (king of Egypt), Miriam (Moses' sister), Aaron (Moses' brother), Joshua (Moses' successor)

Claim to fame: The story of God delivering the Israelites from Egypt through miraculous plagues and the parting of the Red Sea, not to mention the Ten Commandments

Place in the Bible: Second book of Law in the Old Testament

POST-GENESIS

The book of Exodus picks up the story line where the book of Genesis ended. At the end of Genesis the twelve sons of a man named Israel had come to live in Egypt. They did this because of a famine in their own land. They were able to do this because one brother, Joseph, had built his home and a great reputation in Egypt, so his brothers were welcome.

Once there, the family of Israel grew and grew. They became a small nation among the Egyptians, and that was nerve-racking for Pharaoh. What if they decided to overthrow the government? Because of his fears, he made the Israelites slaves. Thus began a very dark time in the history of the Israelites.

Even as slaves, the nation of Israel continued to grow. (This had been promised by God to the very first ancestor of the Jewish nation, Abraham.) Pharaoh tried another form of population control: he let the female infants live and destroyed the male infants. In the midst of this tragedy, God raised up a leader named Moses, who would eventually stand up for his people and lead them to freedom.

Most of Exodus is about that journey to freedom, from Egypt, through the desert, to the Promised Land. The journey of the Israelites was a lot like the journey of a Christian: we are saved from the slavery of sin, we travel through an often difficult desert of a life, and then finally we get to our real home, heaven.

MOSES

Moses is the main character in Exodus (after God Himself, that is).

Moses was born into a courageous family. When he was born there was a decree from the king that all male babies should be destroyed. Moses' mom hid him for three months, then made a floating basket and hid him in the basket at the banks of the Nile River. His sister, Miriam, stood watch.

When the princess came to bathe in the river, she found the basket and adopted the contraband Israelite baby. It was she who gave him the name Moses (which means "out of the water"). Moses' sister, Miriam, showed quick wit and great timing. When the princess found baby Moses, Miriam immediately offered to go and find a Hebrew "babysitter." She brought back Moses' very own mother.

Moses grew up in the palace but as a young man was exiled from Egypt. (He killed an Egyptian for mistreating an Israelite.) It was during this time of exile that God carved out Moses' life's mission: to free His people, to lead them back to Canaan, their promised land, and to establish the Ten Commandments on the way. Easy enough? You thought YOU had it rough. . . .

Sure enough, Moses did lead the people out of Egypt and to the border of their homeland. It took him over forty years to do it and stress points galore, but he died a man who had seen God's promise come true.

NUMBERS, NUMBERS, NUMBERS

How many commandments? (10)
How many years wandering in the desert? (40)
How many plagues? (10)
How many Hebrews left Egypt? (600,000 men, not to mention women and children)

How many plagues can you name? There were ten. . . .
1. Water to blood
2. Frogs, frogs, and more frogs
3. Biting insects
4. Swarms of flies
5. The plague on the Egyptian cattle
6. Boils or sores
7. Hailstorms
8. Locusts (plant-eating insects)
9. Three days of darkness
10. Death of the firstborn

Which of these plagues were NOT a part of Moses' request of Pharaoh?
❏ extreme dandruff
❏ bad hair days
❏ sunburn
❏ numbness of the mouth like Novocain induces
❏ weeklong visits from mother-in-laws
❏ allergic reactions to sand

THE PASSOVER

One of the most precious rituals of the Jewish faith finds its origins in the tenth plague Moses pronounced on Egypt. During the plague, the angel of death swept through Egypt, taking the lives of the firstborn sons. The Israelites were instructed to smear the blood of a lamb on their doorposts. If they did so, their firstborn sons were spared. There is a special meal associated with the Passover. Today we often call the celebration of that meal a "seder."

The last meal that Jesus shared with His disciples before His crucifixion was a Passover meal.

The Passover is a beautiful symbol of Jesus Christ's sacrifice for the sins of His people: the innocent lamb, the shed blood, the sacrifice of the firstborn.

STORIES FROM THE ROAD

A lot of amazing things happened to the Israelites along their journey. Here are some favorites among the "remember whens."

Bread from heaven. The people were in a DESERT for much of the trip. Each morning a breadlike substance would be lying on the ground like snow. This is how they ate (Exodus 16:2–4).

The quail. Once when the people were craving meat, quail came "out of nowhere" to supply a barbecue feast (Exodus 16:13).

Water. Once it came from a rock (Exodus 17:2–7), and once a bitter stream turned sweet just for the Israelites' drinking (Exodus 15:22–25).

Navigation. The people were led by a cloud by day and a pillar of fire by night. No need to ask directions when God is leading (Exodus 13:21–22).

The Ten Commandments. God Himself wrote these on stone. Remember, this was before printing presses and electricity. Writing ten commands in stone was no little feat (Exodus 20).

Moses' glow. After Moses had spent time with God on the mountain, his face literally glowed. He had to wear a veil so the people could deal with him without being distracted (Exodus 34:29–35).

Leviticus

A HOLINESS INSTRUCTION MANUAL

The Israelites (descendants of Abraham through his grandson Israel) organized themselves as they journeyed from their lives as slaves in Egypt to settlers in their own land. They assigned roles, they trained some administrative assistants, they ordained priests, they divided land. One family, the descendants of Levi, were assigned to be priests. They cared for the tabernacle (a portable temple). They helped with the sacrifices. They "kept house." They cared for the precious artifacts that reminded their people of the journey to freedom.

The book of Leviticus is a how-to manual for Israel's priests. It is a detailed instruction booklet for just about any situation that might arise. Keep in mind that the Israelites at this time could have been described as vagabonds: They lived in tents, and they moved often. Sanitation was a big concern. The priests were responsible for teaching the people what was "clean" and what was "unclean." There were guidelines regarding mildew, leprosy, disease, food, sin, sacrifices, and even holidays.

Leviticus is a practical treatise on how to worship, how to live in community, and how to stay alive. Don't let the fancy-shmancy Latin-sounding name fool you. In the situation for which it was written, Leviticus is the most practical of books: rubber-meets-the-road kind of stuff.

HOLINESS

The information found in Leviticus kept the people healthy and clean, but it also taught them something about God. It taught them that God is holy. First, this means that He is clean and without imperfection. Next, it means He is one-of-a-kind, different from anything else.

SACRIFICES

From the earliest historical records, animal sacrifices were a part of religious life. The concept of an innocent shedding its blood to atone for someone's bad deeds was a part of Jewish and Gentile history alike. (See Genesis 4:4–5.)

Leviticus gives specific guidelines for sacrifices: what animals, what kind, when, and how. Sacrifices did involve blood and a certain amount of brutality. They were a picture of the sacrifice that Jesus Christ eventually made for all of us; He in His innocence shedding His blood for our bad deeds. The sacrifices were an appalling demonstration of just how seriously God regards our sin.

Numbers

VITAL STATISTICS

Name: Numbers. This name comes from the census taken of the Israelites in chapters 1–3 and 26. The Jewish people actually called this book by its first word, which in Hebrew meant "in the wilderness."

When written: 1450–1410 B.C. (3,450 years ago)

Author: Moses

Kind of book: A log or record kept over time to record facts and events

In a nutshell: The Israelites journeyed through the wilderness because they failed to believe God would do what He promised.

Names you might recognize: Moses, Aaron, Miriam, Joshua, Caleb, Balaam and a talking donkey

Place in the Bible: Fourth book of Law in the Old Testament

A CAPTAIN'S LOG

Numbers is a book of facts, figures, and events. It is a record, kept by Moses, of thirty-eight years of wandering.

The Israelites had been delivered out of Egypt by God Himself through miracle after miracle. (For instance, food that came like dew every morning and water that gushed out of rocks.) After two years of miracles and hardships, their journey was about to come to a wonderful end—or so they thought.

The Israelites sent twelve spies into Israel to scope out just how big a task lay ahead in reclaiming the land. When the spies returned, ten of them were overwhelmed with fear. Only two of the spies, Joshua and Caleb, remembered what God had already brought them through and said, "We can do it, with God's help."

After all God had done, the people doubted Him and were afraid to enter. Because of the people's lack of faith, they wandered for forty more years before trying again. In fact, everyone who was over twenty when they left Egypt died before entering Israel—except Joshua and Caleb.

NUMBSKULL AWARDS

In many ways, Numbers is a book about failures: foolishness, acts of indiscretion, lack of judgment, poor choices, and just plain old sin. Here are the top five winners for foolish choices recorded in Numbers.

5. Korah (Numbers 16). Korah got two buddies and 250 henchmen and staged an insurrection against Moses. Know what happened? The earth swallowed up Korah.

4. The prophet Balaam (Numbers 22–24). Balaam was paid by King Balak (honorable mention in the Numbskull Awards) to put a curse on Israel. God interceded even to the point of making Balaam's own donkey try to reason with him. Can't get much worse than that.

3. Miriam and Aaron (Numbers 12). Leave it to family. Moses' own sister and brother decided they wanted a bigger piece of the power. Instead, all Miriam got was a temporary case of leprosy, and all they both got was a bigger piece of humble pie.

2. The ten fearful spies (Numbers 13–14). These men were the leaders of their clans. They had witnessed God's provision. Yet they turned chicken when they were within reach of what God had promised. They used their influence to destroy the faith of their people.

1. The people (Numbers 11, 13–14). The all-time prize has to go to the Israelite people. Sure, it's not easy to trek through a desert, but God had been faithful. Out of 600,000 plus, all but two of them doubted God. They worshipped idols, they wished for captivity, they figuratively spit in God's face. These tactics didn't work well for them.

FROM GRATITUDE TO GRUMBLING

The Israelites had been slaves in Egypt for generations. They had prayed long and hard for deliverance. When God allowed them to escape, they rejoiced, and when He provided food and guidance in the desert, they were grateful. . .at first.

"Some troublemakers among them wanted better food, and soon all the Israelites began complaining. They said, 'We want meat! We remember the fish we ate for free in Egypt. We also had cucumbers, melons, leeks, onions, and garlic. But now we have lost our appetite; we never see anything but this manna!'" (Numbers 11:4–6 NCV).

"And all the sons of Israel grumbled against Moses and Aaron; and the whole congregation said to them, 'Would that we had died in the land of Egypt! Or would that we had died in this wilderness! And why is the LORD bringing us into this land, to fall by the sword? Our wives and our little ones will become plunder; would it not be better for us to return to Egypt?'" (Numbers 14:2–3 NASB).

"Why have you brought us up out of Egypt to die in the desert? There is no bread! There is no water! And we detest this miserable food!" (Numbers 21:5).

Numbers shows us what happens to grateful hearts that experience tough times and lose faith in God.

Deuteronomy

FAMOUS LAST WORDS

This book was written at a significant time. The Israelites had traveled for FORTY YEARS in the desert. They did this knowing that one day they would enter the land that had been promised to Abraham, their ancestor. When they had left Egypt (where they were slaves), there were over 600,000 people in the group over the age of twenty. By the time that Deuteronomy describes, just before they enter the land, only three of those people were still living (Moses, Joshua, and Caleb). A whole generation, the ones who had seen God's provision and heard His laws, had passed away. A new generation (or two) had arisen who only knew what they had heard second- or third-hand.

The people are finally at the border. Moses knows he won't get to enter the land with them, and so he must share his heart before he says good-bye. It's his last chance to remind them of God's miraculous provision and of the journey on which He had led them. Moses' last words to his people make up the bulk of Deuteronomy.

PLAYING THE GAME OF REMEMBER WHEN. . .

You know how it is— you sit around with friends and tell stories you all have lived through, just for the fun of reliving them. Remember when we thought we were buying plaster to fix the wall and it was cement instead? Remember when Uncle Dan dressed up for a masquerade party as a go-go dancer and construction workers whistled at him? Remember when we got goofy at the wedding reception and laughed punch right out of our noses?

The remember whens for the Israelites were on a little grander scale, but Moses was still creating the same effect. Remember when God did this for us? Here are some of the Israelites' remember whens.

Remember when the angel of death swept through Egypt but our sons were saved because of the lamb's blood on the doorpost?

Remember when God literally pulled back the waters so we could cross the Red Sea?

Remember when we needed food and it appeared like dew on the ground every morning?

Remember when we needed water and it gushed right out of a hard rock?

Remember when Moses came down from the mountain and his face glowed from God's presence?

Remember when we made that gold calf idol and Moses was so angry he threw down the Ten Commandments tablets and broke them?

Remember when we whined and complained and began to die of poisonous snake bites?

Remember when we heard the report of the spies and were too scared to enter the land?

PUT YOURSELF IN IT

Think about it! A whole generation passed while they were traveling in this gypsy type of environment. Here's one way to look at it.

Let's say you were eight years old when the people left Egypt. You would have left Egypt with your parents and grandparents. By the time you were ten you would have traveled to the border of your destination. Then, when everyone got scared to cross the border, you would have started traveling again, like gypsies in the desert. You would grow to be a teenager, into your twenties, possibly marry and have kids, then into your thirties then into your forties, losing your grandparents and then your parents along the way.

Finally when you are getting close to fifty years old, you return again to the border of that land. You are an adult now, and you're back at the same place you were when you were ten years old. And somehow you've got to

SOUND ADVICE

Moses gave a lot of down-to-earth advice in his last words to the people. Here are some highlights.

- Love God with all your heart (Deuteronomy 6:5).
- Even if someone seems to have special powers, but they diminish your commitment to God, don't follow them (Deuteronomy 13:1–4).
- Don't eat something that died a natural death (Deuteronomy 14:21).
- The purpose of tithing is to teach you always to put God first in your lives (Deuteronomy 14:23).
- Take care of the poor and the people who spend their lives helping others (Deuteronomy 14:29).
- Remember our big holidays. Always get together to celebrate them. They will remind you of what God has done for you (Deuteronomy 16:1–4, 16).
- Don't give God less than your best (Deuteronomy 17:1).
- Never believe a rumor or put a man to death based on only one witness's testimony (Deuteronomy 17:4–7).
- Help each other take care of your property (Deuteronomy 22:1–3).
- Adultery is a life-and-death matter. Don't take it lightly (Deuteronomy 22:22).
- Don't charge interest to your own countrymen (Deuteronomy 23:19–20).
- Do business honestly (Deuteronomy 25:13–16).

keep from making the same mistakes your parents did.

It DOES sound like a good time for a book like Deuteronomy: a book that says, "Okay, this is where we've come from and what we are about and where we are going. We've spent forty years making mistakes. Let's regroup and move ahead."

THE PROBLEM WITH THE ISRAELITES

The Israelites had a once-in-a-lifetime experience. There is probably no other time when God's presence was more evident every day. There was a pillar of fire and a cloud that led the people. They saw miracle after miracle: food on the ground every morning, quails out of thin air, water out of rocks, divine plagues and punishments. God was obviously present and working.

Yet the Israelites continued to doubt.

It would be easy to judge these people, to say they had it easy. After all, they didn't have to have a lot of faith; they could see God's actions right before their eyes.

It might have been easier to see God work, but the Israelites only show us basic human nature. Most of us have experienced some kind of answered prayer, only to worry during the next time of trouble whether God will answer us. Most of us have seen God work in some way, whether we called it a miracle, guidance, or intuition. Yet we didn't trust that we'd ever see Him work again.

The Israelites show us that we all are capable of not trusting God, and of asking Him to continually prove Himself to us.

MOSES' DEATH

Moses led an amazing life. He was one of the few Israelite males his age to survive a royally decreed slaughter. He was raised in a palace when he should have been a slave. He spent forty years living in the desert in preparation for this journey and more than forty years wandering the desert during the journey.

He spent his life following God's call and leading his people from slavery to freedom and a land promised to them. But at the end of it all, he never set foot in that land. He first knew this would happen when God gave him a simple set of instructions and, for once, Moses didn't obey them. The people needed water and God told Moses to speak to a rock and water would come. In frustration and anger, though, Moses didn't just speak to the rock; he violently and angrily struck the rock. He took on himself what was only God's to do. He lost perspective.

We don't know for now why a man who did so many good things still had this one thing held against him. It's one of the questions we won't have answered for us in this life. But Moses lived a good life and was an honorable man. The Bible calls Moses the humblest man on earth.

DEUTERONOMY IN A NUTSHELL

"This day I call the heavens and the earth as witnesses against you that I have set before you life and death, blessings and curses. Now choose life, so that you and your children may live and that you may love the LORD your God, listen to his voice, and hold fast to him. For the LORD is your life, and he will give you many years in the land he swore to give to your fathers, Abraham, Isaac and Jacob" (Deuteronomy 30:19–20).

Joshua

JOSHUA THE SOLDIER

Way back when the Israelites were being held in Egypt as slaves, they had
enough on their figurative plate just thinking about getting out of town. God
worked plenty of miracles to help them out of the city limits and across the
desert to their destination. When they got there, a stark realization hit them:
"We left here a long time ago. Other people have settled here now, and if we
want our homeland back, we are going to have to run these people off! And
these people are very large." This realization, and the fear that arose from it,
kept the people from entering their homeland.

After forty more years of wandering, they faced the border again. This
time, though, they had a different kind of leader. God had given them Joshua,
a soldier and a strategist.

The book of Joshua is about the battles the Israelites waged to recapture
and resettle their land. It involves a lot of force and a lot of blood. It involves
a lot of actions that our present culture considers barbaric and violent. It was
a barbaric and violent time.

Looking beyond those cultural differences, it is a story of faith. When the people trusted in God's strength and obeyed His commands, they won their battles. When they didn't, they lost (and lost miserably). In this way, the book of Joshua is relevant to the battles we face today in our lives, even though our weapons and our enemies look a lot different.

TRUTH IS STRANGER THAN FICTION

The Israelites won their battles as much by miracle as by strategy. Here are a few miracles God performed:

- They cross a river—on dry ground (Joshua 3:9–17).
- The people shout and the walls around a city fall down (Joshua 6:1–27).
- God instructs Joshua to fake a retreat and stage an ambush (Joshua 8:15–29).
- God wins a battle with a hailstorm (Joshua 10:6–11).
- The sun literally stands still so there's more time to fight (Joshua 10:13–14).

Judges

VITAL STATISTICS

Name: Judges. Before Israel had a king, the rulers were called judges.
When written: We don't know.
Author: Some people think Samuel wrote it, but no one is sure.
Kind of book: Judges is a narrative, or story, that teaches us about history.
The judges: Othniel, Ehud, Shamgar, Deborah, Gideon, Tola, Jair, Jephthah, Ibzan, Elon, Abdon, Samson
Place in the Bible: Second book of History in the Old Testament

THE BOOK OF JUDGES

Before the Israelites were slaves in Egypt, they were just a family with twelve sons led by their father, Israel. When they left Egypt after generations of slavery, they were a people of over 600,000 adults led by a countryman, Moses. As they were settling into their land, they were led by a soldier, Joshua. Once they settled, they spent some time without any leadership at all. It is this period of time that the book of Judges describes.

The era of the judges was an era of repeated cycles in the lives of the Israelites. They would fall away from God and fall prey to their enemies. When things got bad enough, they would turn back to God and He would raise up a leader, called a judge (often a military leader), who would rescue them from their current dilemma. But as the cycle continued, the people would fall away again as soon as that judge had died or lost his or her influence. This cycle repeated itself through at least twelve different judges.

DEBORAH

Deborah is one of the most famous judges, and the only one we know of who was a woman. She was wise and discerning and a prophet of God. She was known for holding court and settling disputes under a palm tree.

One day she informed Barak, a military leader, that he was to organize 10,000 men to wage a war. Barak refused to go to war unless Deborah accompanied him. Deborah's response was very interesting. She reminded Barak that if she went with him to war, the word would be spread that a woman won the battle. (Remember, this was a VERY sexist era. This interchange, alone, required Deborah and Barak to live above the culture of their day.)

Deborah did go to battle with Barak, and they were victorious. Their song of victory is recorded in Judges 5.

GIDEON

Gideon was an unlikely leader. He wasn't a member of an important family, and he wasn't even an important member of his own family. But God called him to lead and he obeyed.

Gideon started with 32,000 men. Through God's leadership, he pared them down to just 10,000. Through testing that 10,000, he pared them down to just 300 men. With just 300 men Gideon accomplished God's purposes.

At one point in Gideon's life he needed to know God's direction, so he created a little test. He put a fleece of wool out on the ground overnight and asked God to let dew fall on the fleece but not on the ground. God did it. The next night Gideon asked God to let dew fall on the ground but not on this fleece. God did it. Today people still talk about putting a fleece out before God to determine a specific answer or to "find His will" about something. When they do, they are referring to Gideon.

SAMSON

Samson is, perhaps, the most famous judge. He grew to be the strongest man in the country. His strength was founded on a special commitment he had made to God, called a Nazirite commitment. Part of this promise requires that the Nazirite never cut his hair. As long as Samson kept this commitment, his strength stayed with him.

He got involved with a woman named Delilah, though. She tricked him into cutting his hair. Samson's life went from bad to worse from then on. He was blinded and kept as a slave. He eventually killed himself along with his captors.

The culture during the time of the judges may have been very different from our own, but human nature wasn't. Sometimes life is easy and we go our own way. But then something turns us back to God and we follow Him and find victory in Him. Soon enough, it seems, we are off doing our own thing again.

The Israelites are a reminder to us to turn back to God often and soon rather than waiting for disaster or a need to be rescued.

Ruth

A LOVE STORY

The book of Ruth is about love on a lot of different levels. The story opens with a woman, Naomi, her husband, and her two sons leaving their home because of famine. They settled in a land named Moab. There the two boys married. (Their wives were named Orpah and Ruth.) Naomi, Orpah, and Ruth all became widows. After the deaths of her husband and her sons, Naomi decided to go back to her hometown and freed her daughters-in-law to go and make their own lives in their own land.

After much protesting, Naomi finally convinced Orpah to leave, but Ruth would not budge. She committed to building her life with Naomi. Together they traveled back to Bethlehem. Their experiences there are told in the book of Ruth.

THE REST OF THE STORY

After settling in Bethlehem, Ruth went out to gather leftover wheat from the fields surrounding Bethlehem. She was noticed by a distant relative of Naomi named Boaz. According to Jewish laws, he could marry Ruth and at the same time actually be honoring a family obligation.

That's exactly what happened. Ruth and Boaz married and gave Naomi a grandchild. And (get a load of this) it was through their family line that the famous King David, as well as Jesus Christ, was born.

I DO

In many weddings the bride and groom say these words to each other. There are also wedding songs that use these words for lyrics. In reality, though, these are the words that Ruth said to her mother-in-law, Naomi, when Ruth refused to leave Naomi.

"Don't urge me to leave you or to turn back from you. Where you go I will go, and where you stay I will stay. Your people will be my people and your God my God" (Ruth 1:16).

1 Samuel

FIRST, THE STORY OF A PRIEST

Samuel was a miracle baby. His mother had been infertile and prayed long and hard for a child. Because she was so aware that her child was a gift from God, when he was old enough, she sent him to live at the temple to be raised and apprenticed by Eli, the priest.

When Samuel grew up he was the leader of Israel. But what Israel wanted was a king. A king?! This would change everything about Israel's government. They had only been ruled by God and then a few judges (see the book of Judges). Samuel tried to dissuade them, but Israel demanded. They wanted to be like all the other countries around them (a logic you might recognize from an argument with a middle schooler). So it was Samuel who anointed their first and second kings.

NEXT, THE STORY OF A KING

The first king of Israel was a young man named Saul. He had a lot going for him and did many great things for Israel. He was committed to God. . .at first. Then he wavered, then he fell, and then he literally went insane.

During King Saul's most troubled moments, he was calmed by a young musician named David. (Do you remember that old spiritual "Little David, Play on Your Harp"?) David became best friends with Jonathan, Saul's son. Little did Saul know that because he had stopped obeying God, he would one day be replaced by David.

As Saul began to realize David's growing popularity, he became jealous and angry and increasingly distressed. He treated David like an outlaw. King Saul finally died in a battle along with his son, Jonathan.

THE STORY OF ANOTHER KING

David was anointed future king while he was still a young and very unlikely candidate. He was anointed by Samuel.

Soon after, David was honored with the opportunity to play music before King Saul. The king was so impressed with him that he made David an armor-bearer. This is how it came to be that David was at the camp when Goliath made his challenge. You probably remember the story about little David taking his slingshot out to meet the giant Goliath and killing him with one stone.

This was the beginning of David's leadership, but it was the beginning of the end for Saul's. As the story of David and Goliath grew, the people of Israel started comparing David and Saul. Eventually Saul resented it so much that David was left a refugee, an outlaw, wandering from cave to cave trying to survive against Saul's anger and his armies.

When Saul was killed in battle, David sincerely grieved for him. Then David took over the throne.

ROLL CALL

The book of 1 Samuel has enough chariot chases and enough melodrama to be shown in any theater as an action/adventure flick. See the sidebar for what the casting call might look like.

 AUDITIONS OPEN FOR AN UPCOMING ACTION/ADVENTURE SAGA

Title: *The Book of First Samuel*

Hannah—A young mother, full of faith and struggling with infertility; mother of Samuel; seamstress

Elkanah—The slightly insensitive husband of Hannah; responds to her struggle with infertility by asking, "Don't I mean more to you than ten sons?"

Child Samuel—A child loved by his mother but sent to live with strangers in the temple

Youth Samuel—A young man having grown up in the temple, apprenticed by a priest, having heard God's call in the night

Adult Samuel—A leader of a nation; a liaison between the Israelites and God; an advisor to kings

Eli—The old man who raised Samuel, the leader of a nation, but couldn't control his own sons

Saul—A ruler torn apart by his inner demons

Jesse—Father of David, unaware of the special gifts of his youngest son who later became king

David—A young man with integrity and a sense of right groomed by God for the monarchy

2 Samuel

 VITAL STATISTICS

Name: 2 Samuel, because it continues the story begun in 1 Samuel. (Originally these two were one book.)
When written: 930 B.C., just after King David's reign
Author: We don't know for sure, but the book includes some writings of Nathan and Gad just like 1 Samuel does. The priest Samuel had died during the events described in 1 Samuel.
Kind of book: This is a narrative. It tells events chronologically, just as they happened.
In a nutshell: Tells the story of Israel while David was the king
Place in the Bible: Fifth book of History in the Old Testament

STORY OF A MONARCHY

The book of 2 Samuel is a continuation of the story begun in the book of 1 Samuel. At the end of 1 Samuel, King Saul had been killed in battle and King David had taken the throne. Second Samuel is all about King David's monarchy.

THE RISE OF DAVID

David was an interesting character. The only other person the Bible has more stories about is Jesus Christ. David was a great man, but not always a good one. He often stood for right, but he often failed as a husband and father.

The first ten chapters of 2 Samuel are about the great things that King David did. He built a strong and prosperous kingdom. He returned the ark of the covenant to the tabernacle. He made plans to build a temple. He kept a lifelong promise to his best friend, Jonathan (who died in battle with King Saul), and took care of Jonathan's physically challenged son.

THE FALL OF DAVID

David's most famous mistake (and the beginning of his fall from power) was an affair he had with a married woman named Bathsheba. First, David pursued her, slept with her, and then found out she had become pregnant. Next he tried to get her husband, Uriah, home from war so he would think the baby was his. Poor Uriah (besides having an awful name by today's standards) so revered the king that he wouldn't even go home and enjoy his wife while he was on leave.

Next, David set Uriah up to be killed in battle. So David was guilty of adultery, attempted paternity fraud, and murder—all from seeing someone

A GREAT FLICK

The book of 2 Samuel functions as a sequel to 1 Samuel. If 1 Samuel was an action/adventure movie, then 2 Samuel would be an action/thriller. This would be the cast of 2 Samuel.

King David—Fully king and fully man, the passage of his life runs the gamut between elated with worship and torn with grief

Mephibosheth—Physically challenged from a childhood accident, this would-be prince knows the fear and humility of being the underdog

Michal—The daughter of a king; the wife of another king; royalty from the inside out. This character knows how to express her displeasure and get what she wants

Bathsheba—A woman, beautiful and, perhaps, naive

Nathan—The prophet who speaks the truth even at the risk of danger to himself

Amnon—The young and selfish prince who takes what he wants, when he wants it, and leaves the cleanup to everyone else

Tamar—The victim/princess who leaves the standing-up-for-herself to someone else

Absalom—The young, impetuous, rebellious prince, capable of killing a brother in a rage and trying to overthrow his father as king

bathing and giving in to temptation. This is a king?

David ended up making Bathsheba his wife, but the baby died. They later had more children—including the future king, Solomon.

THE DYSFUNCTIONAL FAMILY OF DAVID

After David's affair with Bathsheba, his life only went from bad to worse. His children by his first wives were out of control. One son, Amnon, raped his half sister, Tamar. Another son, Absalom (who had supermodel good looks and long hair), killed Amnon because of the rape. Eventually Absalom rebelled against his father. He was killed by King David's men when they found him hanging from a tree limb by his hair. His mule had ridden under the tree, and when Absalom's hair caught in the limbs, the mule just kept on going (yes, it really happened).

David's throne was succeeded by his son Solomon. Solomon was the second-born son of Bathsheba and grew to be a wise and wealthy king.

1 Kings

 VITAL STATISTICS

Name: 1 Kings. (The books of 1 and 2 Kings were originally one book.)

When written: We really don't know.

Author: We aren't sure, but it might have been written by a group of people.

Kind of book: A record or narrative of chronological events. (If this were a movie, it would be a political thriller.)

In a nutshell: The tales of the kings of Israel and Judah after King David

Claim to fame: The account of Solomon, the wisest and richest king of Israel

Place in the Bible: Sixth book of History in the Old Testament

THE STORY LINE

The book of 1 Kings opens with the death of the great King David. Before he died, David named one of his sons, Solomon, as his successor. The first half of 1 Kings is about Solomon establishing his kingdom, building the temple, and amassing his unimaginable wealth.

The second half of 1 Kings is about the kingdom after Solomon. Things get a little complicated here, so hang on tight. The one kingdom of Israel divides into two kingdoms (Israel and Judah), sort of an ongoing civil war.

It might sound like things were really changing for the people of Israel (who are now known as the people of Israel and the people of Judah), but in reality it's the same song, second verse. They still are falling away from God until they get in trouble and then running back to Him for help. God forgives and helps them, but He doesn't protect them from consequences, and by the end of the story, those consequences are pretty grim.

KING SOLOMON

Solomon was known for his wisdom. In fact, God appeared to Solomon in a dream and told him to ask for anything he wanted. (Who wouldn't love to be in that dream? The God of all creation offering you anything. . .) Solomon's request was a surprising one. He asked for wisdom to rule well and to know right from wrong. God rewarded such a request by giving Solomon not only wisdom and understanding, but also the wealth and honor that he didn't ask for.

One of the first things Solomon did as king was build a beautiful temple. Solomon then built his own palace (took thirteen years) and continued to amass amazing wealth. Sounds great, right? Well, there was one little problem.

ONE LITTLE PROBLEM

Way back when, Solomon had married a foreigner, a girl from Egypt (where his forefathers had been slaves, you might note). Along with this wife came her religious practices of worshipping idols. He also married many other women who worshipped many other gods. Wouldn't you know it, while things were going great for Solomon, he got more and more tolerant of these idol-worship practices until Solomon himself was worshipping false gods! It was like spitting in the face of God Almighty.

By the end of Solomon's life, he was a disillusioned old man. He had let go of his foundation and his kingdom went right downhill after him.

THE DIVIDED KINGDOM

You might remember that the origin of the twelve tribes of Israel was the twelve sons of Jacob, whom God renamed Israel. They all traveled to Egypt and then traveled back to the land of, you got it, Israel. One tribe, the descendants of Levi, were given no land because they were the priests and would work in the temple rather than work the land. The land was divided among the other eleven tribes.

After Solomon's death, a civil conflict broke out. The northern ten tribes followed a man named Jeroboam. The southern tribes, Benjamin and Judah, continued to follow Solomon's son Rehoboam. They never reunited.

AHAB AND JEZEBEL

You've probably heard of King Ahab and his wife, Queen Jezebel. You may have even heard of someone referred to as a Jezebel. If so, you probably steered clear of them. Jezebel was a mess. She was the Cruella DeVille of her day. If she had lived in the southern kingdom, she'd have probably been called a "floozy." Ahab wasn't a lot better, but he didn't come across quite as conniving. You know. . .behind every bad man, there is usually a worse woman.

Ahab reigned for twenty-two years. The Bible says he considered the sins of the former kings trivial. In fact, the Bible says that Ahab did more to provoke God's anger than all the kings before him. He and his wife reveled in the worship of Baal. They were downright evangelistic (if not Hitler-istic) about it. Basically they encouraged evil as much as they could.

There was one man who stood in their way. An important player in the story of 1 Kings is the prophet Elijah, a beacon in that dark day and an aggravating flea in Jezebel's proverbial mane.

ELIJAH

Elijah was a Tishbite (funny word, say it out loud). He was from a place called Tishbe. He first appeared when he announced to King Ahab that God was about to declare a drought.

Elijah didn't always come out on top. Once in particular he got the "poor-me-willies" when he had worked really hard to confront evil and all he got for it was run out of town. But most often Elijah had great faith, and God used him and provided for him in miraculous ways. He was fed by ravens once. A widow's flour and oil were miraculously replenished because she fed him. It was even through Elijah that a woman's son was brought back to life. But there is definitely one miracle that is Elijah's all-time claim to fame.

TALK ABOUT POLITICS

As wise as Solomon was, his son Rehoboam was that unwise. In fact, the division of the kingdom of Israel came about this way. . . .

When Rehoboam took over the leadership of the country, it was still a whole, united country. His main political rival, Jeroboam, stirred up the people and they came to the new young king with this request: "Your father worked us too hard. Lighten our load." Rehoboam asked them to come back in three days and he would give them his answer.

He went immediately to some wise old advisors. Sounds good so far, right? The advisors told him, "You'd better listen to them, or you'll have trouble on your hands."

Rehoboam then went to his peers, his young advisors, and they told him, "You tell those people they haven't seen anything yet!" In other words, "Let 'em know who's boss!"

You can probably guess whose advice the young king listened to. The people revolted (with a little help from Jeroboam) and thus was the division of the kingdom.

Politics is politics.

THE BIG SHOWDOWN

Elijah invited Ahab and Jezebel's false religion to a showdown once. It was on top of Mount Carmel. He instructed the prophets of Baal (an idol) to build an altar, place a sacrifice there, and pray to their god to send fire down to light the altar. Elijah built an altar as well and soaked it in barrels and barrels of water.

As you can imagine, the Baal prophets prayed and danced and shouted and even (yes, really) cut themselves to show their fervor and sincerity. But when you are praying to nothing, nothing happens. No fire from heaven. Only a lot of bleeding prophets and some very raw meat.

Then Elijah prayed over his wet, soggy sacrifice on the altar. And God responded. Fire came down from heaven and consumed the altar, the sacrifice, and the water.

It was a good day for God's people. It was a bad day for Baal's prophets (who were chased down and killed). And boy, was Jezebel mad.

2 Kings

 VITAL STATISTICS

Name: 2 Kings. (This is a continuation of the story in 1 Kings, the story of the kings of Israel and Judah.)
When written: We really aren't sure.
Author: Can't say for sure, but in light of the customs of that day, it might have been a group of writers.
Kind of book: Story or narrative, perhaps even somewhat of a political chronicle
In a nutshell: Tells the story of the kings of Israel and Judah after Jehoshaphat and Ahaziah and during the time of Elijah and Elisha, the prophets. (Yes, there really was a Jehoshaphat—but he probably wasn't called "Jumpin'" by his friends.)
Place in the Bible: Seventh book of History in the Old Testament

SETTING POLICY

The national leadership of a country determines the direction of the whole country, politically and otherwise. Of all the kings below, only two worshipped God.

JUDAH	ISRAEL
Jehoram (2 Kings 8)	Joram (2 Kings 3)
Ahaziah (2 Kings 8)	Jehu (2 Kings 10)
Athaliah (2 Kings 11)	Jehoahaz (2 Kings 13)
Joash (2 Kings 11)	Jehoash (2 Kings 13)
Amaziah (2 Kings 14)	Jeroboam II (2 Kings 14)
Azariah (2 Kings 15)	Zechariah (2 Kings 15)
Jotham (2 Kings 15)	Shallum (2 Kings 15)
Ahaz (2 Kings 16)	Menahem (2 Kings 15)
Hezekiah (2 Kings 18)	Pekahiah (2 Kings 15)
Manasseh (2 Kings 21)	Pekah (2 Kings 15)
Amon (2 Kings 21)	Hoshea (2 Kings 17)
Josiah (2 Kings 22)	
Jehoahaz (2 Kings 23)	
Jehoiakim (2 Kings 23)	
Jehoiakin (2 Kings 24)	
Zedekiah (2 Kings 24)	

A NATION DIVIDED

The book of 2 Kings is a sequel to 1 Kings. Israel had divided into two kingdoms (northern: Israel; southern: Judah) with their own separate kings, separate economies, separate worships, and separate problems.

Throughout the different governments, God sent prophets to call the people back to obedience. Unfortunately, they continued to return to idolatry. In the end, each kingdom fell. The northern kingdom fell to the Assyrians and the southern kingdom fell to the Babylonians.

TWO GOOD KINGS

There were two kings in the southern kingdom that tried to get their country back in line. The first was Hezekiah. One of his first official acts was to restore and open the temple and to destroy the idol altars and worship center. One of his biggest contributions was to create an aqueduct system so that water came within Jerusalem's city walls.

The second righteous king was Josiah. Josiah was crowned king at the age of eight. He also restored the temple and, in doing so, found an old copy of the Book of the Law (probably Deuteronomy). Because of this book, Josiah called himself and his people to a new level of understanding and obedience. Josiah was killed in battle at only thirty-nine years of age.

PROPHETS

During Israel and Judah's time of falling away from God, they were consistently reminded of their mistakes by prophets. These men sometimes foretold the future, but also just told the truth. They spoke with the kings. They were known throughout the land. Often they were respected as well as abused.

One of the most famous prophets was Elijah. Elijah left the earth not through death but through a chariot of fire (a story you allude to every time you sing "Swing low, sweet chariot, comin' for to carry me home").

Elijah's apprentice prophet was Elisha. Elisha lived an honorable life and even established a school for prophets.

THREE SIMPLE RULES

Second Kings and the lives of these kings show us three simple rules.

1. Follow God and, in the long run, life will be better.
2. Don't follow God and, though you might enjoy it now, destruction is on the way.
3. Listen when God speaks. You might think you're doing okay and find out you need some spiffing up.

The work of some of the other prophets of that era is recorded in actual books of the Bible such as Isaiah, Micah, Hosea, and Jeremiah. God showed His love by never giving up on His people. He kept calling them back through the message of the prophets, but they never got it together enough to follow Him.

1 Chronicles

VITAL STATISTICS

Name: 1 Chronicles. (A chronicle is a record, or a history.)
When written: Around 430 B.C.
Author: Ezra wrote this book (according to Jewish tradition).
Kind of book: Some of this book is a narrative, but there are also some genealogies included. (These genealogies can give an impression of borrrrr-ing, but they are good information.)
In a nutshell: First Chronicles covers much of the same history as 2 Samuel but tells us more about the faith of the people than the politics.
Names you might recognize: Samuel, David, Nathan, Solomon
Place in the Bible: Eighth book of History in the Old Testament

A SENSE OF ROOTS IN A DARK TIME

The book of 1 Chronicles was written at a time in Israel's history when the people had been physically displaced from their homes. After their exile they came back home to find that their land had been settled by foreigners. They needed to reunite as a people and reconnect with God. The history of 1 Chronicles is to help them do that.

GENEALOGIES

The book of 1 Chronicles opens with lists upon lists of genealogies. In fact, there are eight chapters of these lists. True, they are not enthralling bedtime fare, but look at them through the eyes of the original readers. This was a culture in which individuals defined themselves by their family history. Their land was even parceled out according to which of the twelve sons of Israel their family descended from. Their whole identity was in genealogies. Their way of life, for the most part, was passed on through stories, oral traditions, and feasts and holidays that found their origin in the great deliverance from Egypt (see Exodus for clarification on that one).

So, while you may not read these genealogies word for word, understand that to these people these lists were the only roots they had. Their homes were reinhabited; their land was full of squatters. All that defined them as a nation were the names you see in 1 Chronicles and the lives those names represented.

ISRAEL'S FAMILY HISTORY

The largest part of 1 Chronicles is a different kind of history. It describes much of the same events you find in 2 Samuel and in 1 and 2 Kings. There is a much different perspective on those events though. First Chronicles was written many years after these events. Whenever you look at a period of time from the vantage point of "many years later," you see things differently. You see more of the highlights than the details. You see the significance rather than just the events themselves. First Chronicles really describes the history of worship in Israel, the history of the people's relationship with God, rather than just who ruled when and for how long.

KING DAVID

David is the central character in 1 Chronicles. As a king, David did many things, but this book describes in most detail his temple preparations.

David focused the pre-exile Israelites on worship. Because of this, it was a good thing for the post-exile Israelites to look back again on David's role in history so that they could, once again, make worship a priority. Their temple lay in ruins. Their homes weren't much better. In 1 Chronicles they could find a pattern to follow to find their roots in their family and in their religious commitment.

ACCOMPLISHMENTS

When we look back on our lives, or anybody's life, we can see a clear path of what they accomplished. But when we are in the middle of living our lives, sometimes the path is not so clear. We can't know what King David was thinking about worship in his day, but looking back it's as if he had this plan in mind:

- Recapture Jerusalem so I can put the temple there.
- Return the ark of the covenant *(the most holy thing in Jewish history, sort of like a holy time capsule)* to the tabernacle. *(The tabernacle was the portable precursor to the temple.)*
- Write songs for the tabernacle choir to sing and work with the choir director, Asaph.
- Organize the priests, the worship musicians, and the guards.
- Gather together building supplies and equipment so that when the time is right, Solomon, my son, can build the temple.

It seems like this must have been David's to-do list because that is exactly what he did.

2 Chronicles

VITAL STATISTICS

Name: 2 Chronicles (a continuation of 1 Chronicles, without the genealogies)
When written: Around 430 B.C.
Author: Ezra wrote this book (according to Jewish tradition).
Kind of book: A chronological recounting of true events
In a nutshell: Recounts the history of the Israelites from Solomon's reign until their captivity in Babylon
Claim to fame: Second Chronicles is another recounting of the events described in 1 and 2 Kings, including the description of the temple.
Place in the Bible: Ninth book of History in the Old Testament

A NATION IN REVIEW

The book of 2 Chronicles is a continuation of 1 Chronicles. So, like 1 Chronicles, it is a recounting of the historical events listed in 1 and 2 Kings, but from a very different perspective. Second Chronicles is written many years later (than Kings) and in the rearview. The Jewish people have been away from their land in exile and are just returning. They have been lost and wandering with no roots and no familiarity.

The writer of the Chronicles (probably Ezra, according to tradition) set about to give the people a sense of history and identity. In light of this, the Chronicles place more emphasis on the positive aspects of the historical characters. There were many wicked and idolatrous kings in the history of Judah, but the Chronicles bring out the best in the reigns of these men. It is a deliberate attempt to remind Israel of what they can be proud of and hold on to about their history. It is also a reminder of how their forefathers served and worshipped God, so that they can get their new life at home off on the right foot.

SOLOMON

The reign of Solomon takes up the first portion of 2 Chronicles. He was wise. He was wealthy. He was influential. He had many wives. He had it all. In his younger years, it served him well. In his older years, it disillusioned him. In fact, he is the writer of a book of the Bible named Ecclesiastes in which he says he's had it all and without God "all" is nothing.

THE KINGS OF JUDAH

After Solomon's reign, the kingdom was divided into the southern kingdom, Judah, and the northern kingdom, Israel. Second Chronicles concentrates on the rulers of Judah. Of those rulers, 2 Chronicles draws a direct correlation between their commitment to God and the success of their kingdom. Throughout their history God told them, "Obey Me and I will bless you; disobey Me and you will not succeed." Second Chronicles reveals in hindsight that what God said was true.

TABLOIDS

Here are some of the headlines you would read if 2 Chronicles had a tabloid following.

- Solomon reduces silver to the worth of a stone (2 Chronicles 1)
- Grandmother kills all her descendants so she can become queen (2 Chronicles 22)
- Child-king crowned at the age of seven (2 Chronicles 24)
- Ahaz, national leader, involved in child sacrifice (2 Chronicles 28)
- King Jehoahaz sets record for shortest reign (2 Chronicles 36)

Ezra

THE MAIN GIST

You may or may not remember that at the end of 2 Chronicles the Jewish people or Israelites had been exiled to Babylon. When the Persians then invaded Babylon, the Persian leader, Cyrus, let the Jewish people return home. This was a good and a bad thing. They had been in Babylon SEVENTY YEARS! Many of the people who first came had died. More than a whole generation had made their home there. Jerusalem, their hometown, was nine hundred miles away and this was before automobiles. (Even in a car on a highway nine hundred miles takes around fifteen hours. Can you imagine on foot?) There was a reluctance among many to take Cyrus up on his offer.

EXILES RETURN WITH ZERUBBABEL

Out of two million, about fifty thousand did choose to travel back to their homeland with a man named Zerubbabel (zuh-RU-buh-bul). Their priority when they got there was to rebuild the temple. The significance of this act was more than just having a place to worship. It was an act of restructuring their relationship with God.

There was a great celebration when the builders completed the foundation. There was music and cheering and worship. And there was sadness, too. The senior citizens who had returned with Zerubbabel could remember the temple that Solomon built, grand and glorious. They wept at how far they had fallen away from those days.

The history of these people had featured a very on-again-off-again style of worship. The fact that they traveled home and rebuilt the temple was a sign that they acknowledged God's leadership in the life of their nation. This was a big step.

EXILES RETURN WITH EZRA

After the temple had been rebuilt, Ezra returned to Jerusalem with about two thousand more people (many of them priests). What he found disappointed him. The temple was together, but was so much less grand than before.

Ezra's main concern wasn't the building though. The temple's poor condition was just a reflection of the poor condition of the people's hearts. This really grieved Ezra. He had a vision for restoring his people. He tore his clothes (which was a sign of grief and despair in those days). He preached his heart out. And it worked! The people renewed their relationship with God.

THERE'S ALWAYS A SNAG IN CONSTRUCTION

Even as long ago as this book records, people used paperwork to delay construction. Observe this scenario from Ezra 4.

- Now remember, there was no e-mail, no fax, no phone, no carbons, no copiers, not even any postal service. There were only camels, chariots, and messengers. And there were nine hundred miles between the building site and the capital city of the government. (You think YOU had delays!)
- Hostile neighbors offer to "help" with construction of the temple. The Israelites refuse their help. The neighbors take the attitude of "We'll show them. . . ."
- The neighbors send messengers or agents with lies about the Israelites. They send these stories back to King Cyrus as long as he reigns, then

King Darius after him.

- They start writing letters. First to King Xerxes, then to King Artaxerxes warning him that the Jewish people are trouble and if the construction continues, they'll probably stop paying taxes. (Ouch. That must have hurt!)
- The king looks up in his files the history of Judah and Israel and sees their history of rebellion. That wasn't reassuring, so he sends back a demand (nine hundred miles again) for the reconstruction to stop.
- But in the midst of this, the Israelites begin to fight fire with fire. They begin construction again and write to the king asking him to look back in his files one more time and find the ORIGINAL decree from King Cyrus authorizing the construction. Off go the secretaries to search through the parchment and stone tablets, and there it is, dust and all. (No building permit EVER took this much work.)
- Construction resumes and the file clerk takes a break.

Nehemiah

 VITAL STATISTICS

Name: Nehemiah, the main character in the historical account
When written: Around 445 B.C.
Author: Nehemiah and Ezra probably collaborated.
Kind of book: Historical narrative, a true story
In a nutshell: Nehemiah returns to Jerusalem to rebuild the walls. (In that day people built their cities on a hill with a wall around for protection. Think of the days of King Arthur.)
Names you might recognize: Nehemiah, Ezra, Sanballat, Tobiah
Place in the Bible: Eleventh book of History in the Old Testament

NEHEMIAH TAKES A RISK

Talk about a career strategy. Nehemiah was a man who believed in a creative job market. As the story opens in this book, Nehemiah is a cupbearer to the king. Part of his job was typical administrative assistant kind of stuff. But part of his job was, literally, to taste the king's wine. One reason was quality control. But the other was poison control. Talk about living on the edge!

The good thing about Nehemiah's job was that it gave him opportunities to talk directly with the king about his concerns. Nehemiah had heard from a friend that the Jewish people who had left Babylon to rebuild Jerusalem were having a bad time. The city walls were destroyed and this left the city open to attack. This news broke Nehemiah's heart.

When the king asked why Nehemiah seemed so sad, there was a ready response. Nehemiah asked for a leave of absence to help build the wall. He got the time off from work and headed to Jerusalem.

NEHEMIAH BUILDS A WALL

A couple of days after his arrival, Nehemiah snuck out at night and surveyed the wall. It was a mess.

To understand why he had to sneak around, you have to understand that this land had been inhabited by so many people that there were mixed feelings in regard to the Jewish people reinhabiting the land. There were also government officials who were very sensitive to any independence the Jewish people might regain that would cause them to rebel or (tell me no!) stop paying taxes.

Once Nehemiah had seen the wall, he announced his plan. He divided the gates and sections of the wall among different people and set them to work. Most of the people were glad to be working. Then again, there were two characters named Sanballat and Tobiah.

Sanballat and Tobiah were threatened by the work the Jewish people were doing. They feared they would lose their own power over the people. So, first, they started intimidating them and putting them down verbally.

Nehemiah prayed.

Then they tried to discourage the workers.

Nehemiah reminded them of God's help.

Then they threatened the workers.

Nehemiah armed the workers and set up battle strategies with them. Basically the builders had a tool in one hand and a weapon in the other. What a way to build a wall!

Then Sanballat and Tobiah threatened to assassinate Nehemiah.

Nehemiah prayed again but he didn't back down.

Believe it or not, those builders finished that wall in less than two months (actually fifty-two days, about seven weeks). This was no small feat considering that it was such a sturdy, wide wall that when they finished they marched on top of it around the city to celebrate.

SPEAKER FOR HIRE

If Nehemiah were living today, he would be a prime candidate to speak at leadership conferences. He was an excellent leader and administrator. If he gave you a handout, his main points would look something like this.

- Pray for wisdom about decisions and opportunities.
- If at all possible, work through the powers that be, the chain of command.
- Survey your task well before beginning work.
- Divide your task into manageable segments and then assign them to people who have an interest in their completion.
- Don't give in to bullies.
- Don't let someone threaten your reputation. Stand on your own integrity.
- Confront problems and people head-on.
- Know what the Bible says and follow its advice.

REVIVAL MEETING

After the completion of the wall, Ezra (same guy from the book of Ezra) read the Law of God to the people. Together they confessed their sin and recommitted themselves to follow God and to worship Him, to take care of the temple, and basically, to clean up their act.

Nehemiah worked for a long time to help the Jewish people, or Israelites, renew and maintain their commitment to God's way of doing things.

Esther

VITAL STATISTICS

Name: Esther, the main character of this account
When written: Around 480 B.C.
Author: Not sure, but Mordecai is a possibility. He was Esther's cousin.
Type of book: Historical narrative. This is a true story.
In a nutshell: Even though she is a part of a minority group, Esther enters a contest to be queen and she wins! Because of this, she is able to ask the king to take care of the Israelite people when they are in danger.
Claim to fame: A book of the Bible in which God's name doesn't appear
Place in the Bible: Twelfth book of History in the Old Testament

GENERALLY SPEAKING

Esther is a story that shows God at work in everyday circumstances. It's a story that affirms for us that coincidences, most often, are not by chance at all.

The events of Esther happened in Babylon while the Israelites (or Jewish people) were in captivity there. They weren't slaves; they were forced immigrants. They could do business and live their lives, but they weren't citizens of Babylon. They were waiting to go home someday.

QUEEN VASHTI

The story opens with a conflict between King Ahasuerus (also called Xerxes) and Queen Vashti. The king was having a wild and raucous party with his friends and called for his wife so he could show off her beauty. The queen refused to come. REFUSED TO COME?! That might not seem like a big deal today, but in that day, it was a very big deal. In fact, it was such a big deal that the king divorced her and opened up a search, a beauty contest of sorts, for a new queen.

That event set the stage for Esther's story.

A SLOW READ?

Who says the Bible is a slow read? In this book alone there is
- a women's libber.
- a beauty pageant.
- an assassination attempt.
- a racial conflict.
- a man hung on the gallows he built for someone else.
- the establishment of a national tradition that has continued for almost 2,500 years.
- a classic victory-of-the-underdog story.
- political intrigue.
- the startling insight that even in the days of the Babylonian Empire there was such a thing as a beauty treatment (and it lasted twelve months).

ENTER ESTHER

Esther was a beautiful girl. She was a Jewish girl. She was also an orphan, so her older cousin Mordecai was like a father to her. Esther was entered in the contest. She won and sure enough rose above the ranks and married the king. Somehow this all happened without the king knowing she was Jewish.

Everything went along fine until. . .Haman.

HAMAN'S PLAN

Haman was a Hitler wannabe. He was a power-hungry fellow who would be happy to exterminate the Jewish people from his country. He was a bigot, a racist, a bully. He particularly disliked Esther's cousin, Mordecai. Mordecai had won the king's favor by uncovering an assassination plot, thus saving the king. Haman didn't like Mordecai's good name one little bit, and it didn't help matters that Mordecai was not a man who bowed down before Haman. Haman made a plan to be rid of the Jewish people, with Mordecai at the top of the list.

But what Haman didn't realize was that the queen herself was a Jew and related to the man he was preparing to persecute. Mordecai went to Esther so that she could talk to the king on his behalf and save her people. This was a scary thing for Esther, but she did it and, in fact, uncovered Haman's plot with Haman right there in the room.

THE END

By the end, justice was done. Haman was hanged on his own gallows. His plan was nixed. Mordecai was honored by the king. Esther remained queen but no longer had to keep her nationality a secret. The Jewish people established a new feast, Purim, celebrated even today where they read together the story of Esther and celebrate God's salvation through their very own queen of Persia.

SUCH A TIME

The crux of the book of Esther comes when Mordecai confronts her fear with this statement: "And who knows but that you have come to your royal position for such a time as this?" (Esther 4:14).

That is when we discover God's call and purpose in our lives—when we realize that God has brought us to where we are for a reason, for "such a time as this."

Job

VITAL STATISTICS

Name: Job (pronounced jOHb), the main person in the story
When written: We don't know.
Author: Job might have written it.
Type of book: Even though the text doesn't rhyme, this book is considered poetic.
In a nutshell: Job was a good man who suffered. This story gives some insight into that troublesome issue.
Claim to fame: Teaches us about Satan and about suffering. Still today people refer to the patience of Job.
Place in the Bible: First book of Poetry in the Old Testament

A PEEK BEHIND ETERNITY'S CURTAIN

We don't often think of God and Satan sitting down for a chat. We know they were once companions. Satan was an angel, for goodness' sake, but then things changed, not for goodness' sake.

We may not think about God and Satan communicating, but that is exactly the way the book of Job opens. Satan is talking to God about Job. He makes the accusation that Job is only faithful to God because Job has a good life. God denies that is true and, in modern terms, tells Satan to go ahead and give it his best shot.

Then Job began to suffer. He suffered loss and illness and poverty and, worst of all, three well-meaning friends.

JOB'S "FRIENDS"

At first Job's friends sat with him, offering comfort with their presence. But eventually they did what so many well-meaning people do when they are around suffering. They tried to figure out why it was happening. And ultimately they came to the question we all come to: "What did Job do to deserve this?"

Even sick, having lost his children and his wealth, everything except his despairing wife, Job stood firm. He had done nothing to deserve all this. That left them with the only other question they could ask: "If he doesn't deserve it, then why is it happening?" Since there was no answer to that question, they just kept badgering Job to fess up. Then finally God spoke.

GOD'S REASONING

The bottom line of God's response was "Who do you think you are?" (A question that we can never answer without first visiting "Who do we think God is?") God reestablished His place in the world, His creation, His sovereignty, His power.

God doesn't answer the question of why there is evil and suffering in the world. Probably because it was answered in the first three chapters of Genesis. But God does say that He is the same when we are suffering or when we aren't. He is loving when we are blessed and He is loving when we are cursed. Our suffering is not a product of His punishment or a way in which His feelings have changed about us. Life is a suffering place.

This is still difficult for us to understand mainly because sometimes God intervenes and keeps suffering from us but sometimes He doesn't. And in the end, whether we understand or not, His being able to make that choice is why we call Him God.

LIFE LESSONS

Job is perhaps one of the most timeless and relevant books of the Bible. Who has not wondered why bad things happen to any kind of people? Here are some highlights of the logic and illogic expressed in Job.

"Behold, happy is the man whom God corrects; therefore do not despise the chastening of the Almighty. For He bruises, but He binds up; He wounds, but His hands make whole" (Job 5:17–18 NKJV).

—Eliphaz, Job's friend, a descendant of Esau

"How can a mortal be innocent before God? Can anyone born of a woman be pure? God is more glorious than the moon; he shines brighter than the stars" (Job 25:4–5 NLT).

—Bildad, Job's friend

"Know this: God has even forgotten some of your sin" (Job 11:6).

—Zophar, Job's friend

"Truly God will never do wrong; the Almighty will never twist what is right" (Job 34:12 NCV).

—Elihu, Job's friend

"Are you still maintaining your integrity? Curse God and die!" (Job 2:9).

—Job's wife

"Though he slay me, yet will I hope in him; I will surely defend my ways to his face" (Job 13:15).

—Job, in the midst of his suffering

Psalms

VITAL STATISTICS

Name: Psalms, which means "songs" or "poems"

When written: Somewhere between 1450 and 590 B.C.

Author: There were many authors, including King David, Asaph (the music director at the temple), King Solomon, and Moses (who led the Israelites out of Egypt and transcribed the Ten Commandments).

Type of book: Poetry and lyrics

In a nutshell: These poems and songs express praise, worship, and confession to God.

Claim to fame: Most of these psalms were meant to be sung. So this book is like a very old hymnal. Also, if you open your Bible as close to the middle as possible, you are probably in the book of Psalms. It's the easiest book to find!

Place in the Bible: Second book of Poetry in the Old Testament

IN GENERAL

The book of Psalms is a collection of poems. Most of these poems are also lyrics to a song. Some call this book the "Book of Praises." Others call it the Greek name, *Psalmoi*, which means "twangings" (like on a harp). Still others call it the Psaltery, which comes from "Psalterion" (songs to be played with a harp). Some just call it "the hymnbook of Solomon's temple."

There are 150 songs in Psalms. Some are about God and some are written directly to God. Some are gloriously happy and worshipful, and some are filled with dejection and rage. The psalms were what any songbook is, a collection of the innermost feelings of people. They are honest. They are full of real-life prayers. They are rubber-meets-the-road, real-life thoughts of people who struggled with and celebrated the same things that every person does.

IN SPECIFIC

The topics of Psalms include the following:

- God's goodness
- God's protection
- God's love
- Anger
- Regret
- Jealousy
- Enemies
- Praise
- Joy
- Wonder
- Funeral dirges

 THINK LIBRARY. . .

The book of Psalms can be divided into five smaller books.
Book #1 (1–41)—Focuses on the relationship between God and people.
Book #2 (42–72)—Focuses on the relationship between God and the nation of Israel (or the Jewish people).
Book #3 (73–89)—Focuses on the relationship between formal worship and God's holiness.
Book #4 (90–106)—Focuses on the earth and everything that is on the earth.
Book #5 (107–150)—Focuses on the Word of God. Within each book there are a variety of subjects including praise, repentance, worship, and prayer.

BUT THEY DON'T RHYME

What's that you say? If they are songs, if they are lyrics, if they are poems, why don't they rhyme? Well, since they were written in another language, one might assume that they rhymed in the other language, just not in English.

No. The style of poetry at that time in the Hebrew culture and language was a whole different way of thinking. Their music was not based on three chords and a chorus the way ours is today.

Their poetry forms were based on the thoughts in the poems. The first line usually expressed the central thought. Then the second line repeated or built on that thought. Often each line then continued to build, but on that same central thought. For instance, Psalm 27 builds this way:

> *The LORD is my light and my salvation;*
> *Whom shall I fear?*
> *The LORD is the strength of my life;*
> *Of whom shall I be afraid?*
> *When the wicked came against me*
> *To eat up my flesh,*
> *My enemies and foes,*
> *They stumbled and fell.*
> *Though an army may encamp against me,*
> *My heart shall not fear;*
> *Though war may rise against me,*
> *In this I will be confident.*
> PSALM 27:1–3 NKJV

DOES ANYONE HERE PLAY AN INSTRUMENT?

Today an orchestra is made up of strings, woodwinds, percussions, some brass. A band is made up of drums, guitars, sometimes keyboards. Musical instruments were used in the Jewish "church services" as well.

Cymbals—There were two types of cymbals: The clashing cymbals were large disks. The resounding cymbals were small disks attached to the thumb and the middle finger.

Flute—Also called a shepherd's pipe. Smaller than the oboe and without a reed.

Harp—A twelve-stringed instrument, held vertically and played with the fingers.

Horns—Also called trumpets, these instruments were made of ram's horns or of hammered metal. They called the people to worship. (They also were the instruments used when the people shouted and the walls of Jericho fell down.)

Lyre—Smaller than the harp, with only ten strings and plucked with a pick. Our modern hammered dulcimer is a distant cousin of the lyre.

Oboe—Often translated as "flute" or "pipe", the word *chalil* means an instrument with double reeds, like an oboe.

Rattle—Also called a sistrum. Often these were made of clay with stones inside to make the rattling rhythm sound. Today similar shakers are made out of plastic or wood and shaped like eggs.

Tambourine—Round like our modern tambourines, but with no "jingles" on the side. This tambourine was used as a small drum.

DANCING BEFORE THERE WERE DISCOTHEQUES

Not only were musical instruments used in the worship services of ancient Israel, but dance also was an integral part of worship and of ceremonies. David danced before the Lord. Miriam danced during a celebration.

The movements were certainly different from much of today's dancing and were not sexual in nature, but movement was an important part of celebrating the God who gives life. Go ahead, think about your blessings and do a little jig.

Proverbs

VITAL STATISTICS

Name: Proverbs, wise sayings (you know, like a Chinese proverb)
When written: Between 970 and 950 B.C., during Solomon's early reign
Author: Solomon wrote a lot of them, but some are attributed to Agur and Lemuel (who, by the way, were Arabs, not Israelites).
Type of book: A collection of wise sayings, Hebrew poetry
In a nutshell: Nuggets of wisdom to help people make everyday choices
Place in the Bible: Third book of Poetry in the Old Testament

SOLOMON'S WISDOM

The book of Proverbs is a collection of wise sayings. It's like a bag of godly-wisdom fortune cookies, minus the cookies. These Proverbs are a good example of Hebrew poetry. Many are couplets (two lines) that express the same thought two different ways. Sometimes they restate and sometimes they give examples by stating the opposite.

Proverbial Examples

The fear of the LORD is the beginning of knowledge:
but fools despise wisdom and instruction.
PROVERBS 1:7 KJV
(See, the second line is the opposite of the first line.)

My son, pay attention to what I say;
turn your ear to my words.
Do not let them out of your sight,
keep them within your heart.
PROVERBS 4:20–21
(These second lines restate the first lines.)

Many are the plans in a person's heart,
but it is the LORD's purpose that prevails.
PROVERBS 19:21

HANDOUTS

If you were teaching a seminar based on the book of Proverbs, here are some of the sessions you might include:

- God's Perspective on Sex
- Having Friends
- Knowing God
- Leadership, God's Way
- Loving Things or Loving People?
- Making Sense of Marriage and Family Issues
- Money Management
- Morality and You
- Time Management
- Using Words Wisely
- Working for a Living

 USING THIS BOOK

Some people read a chapter of Proverbs every day month after month. Since it's broken into thirty-one chapters, there is a daily reading that correlates with every day of the month.

Proverbs is a hodgepodge of truth, but it is a precious book, because you can always find something there that will affect your choices on that very day. It's a book about how you live your life in the details where things can get the most complicated.

Ecclesiastes

VITAL STATISTICS

Name: Ecclesiastes
When written: Around 930 B.C.
Author: Solomon, even though he is not mentioned by name. (There are references, such as "son of David," that seem to refer to Solomon.)
Type of book: You might hear this book referred to as wisdom literature or poetry.
In a nutshell: This is a message from someone who had it all: wealth, fame, women, power. His word to us is that having it all is still empty without God.
Claim to fame: The "There is a time for everything" passage in chapter 3. You might remember the hit song "To Everything (Turn, Turn, Turn) There Is a Season (Turn, Turn, Turn)."
Place in the Bible: Fourth book of Poetry in the Old Testament

THE MAN WHO HAD IT ALL

Remember Solomon? He was King David's son. When he was a young king, God asked him what he wanted, and Solomon said, "Wisdom." God rewarded such a discerning answer by giving him that wisdom as well as wealth and power. For many years Solomon lived a life that honored God.

Before it was all over, though, Solomon had slipped. He had gotten a little complacent. He had let some idolatry and some disillusionment slip into the royal household. It is at this point that it is generally believed that he wrote the book of Ecclesiastes.

A phrase that is used umpteen times in Ecclesiastes is "under the sun." ("umpteen" is a round figure depending on which translation you are using). Another recurring theme is "everything is meaningless."

Solomon should know; he had all the conveniences his culture offered him. And still, everything wasn't enough without God.

THE BIBLE ADDRESSES HAPPINESS

While Ecclesiastes has a lot to say about meaninglessness, it also has some things to say about happiness. If you've never read this book before, check these out:

"I know that there is nothing better for people than to be happy and do good while they live" (Ecclesiastes 3:12).

"Moreover, when God gives someone wealth and possessions, and the ability to enjoy them, to accept their lot and be happy in their toil— this is a gift of God" (Ecclesiastes 5:19).

"When times are good, be happy; but when times are bad, consider this: God has made the one as well as the other. Therefore, no one can discover anything about their future" (Ecclesiastes 7:14).

"Be happy while you are young, and let your heart give you joy in the days of your youth. Follow the ways of your heart and whatever your eyes see, but know that for all these things God will bring you into judgment" (Ecclesiastes 11:9).

One thing you can always say about Ecclesiastes—it gives you something to ponder.

FOR EVERY SEASON

You probably remember that famous passage: a time to "this" and a time to "that." Let's see how much of it you really remember.

There is a time for everything, and a season for every activity under the heavens:

a time to be b___ and a time to die,
a time to plant and a time to up____,
a time to kill and a time to h___,
a time to tear down and a time to b____,
a time to w___ and a time to laugh,
a time to mourn and a time to d____,
a time to scatter stones and a time to g_____ them,

a time to em_____ and a time to refrain from _____,
a time to search and a time to g___ up,
a time to keep and a time to t____ away,
a time to tear and a time to m____,
a time to be silent and a time to s_____,
a time to ____ and a time to hate,
a time for ___ and a time for peace.
ECCLESIASTES 3:1–8

TIME TO CHECK YOUR ANSWERS

There is a time for everything, and a season for every activity under the heavens:

a time to be born and a time to die,
a time to plant and a time to uproot,
a time to kill and a time to heal,
a time to tear down and a time to build,
a time to weep and a time to laugh,
a time to mourn and a time to dance,
a time to scatter stones and a time to gather them,
a time to embrace and a time to refrain from embracing,
a time to search and a time to give up,
a time to keep and a time to throw away,
a time to tear and a time to mend,
a time to be silent and a time to speak,
a time to love and a time to hate,
a time for war and a time for peace.
ECCLESIASTES 3:1–8

Song of Solomon

VITAL STATISTICS

Name: Song of Solomon or Song of Songs
When written: Between 970 and 950 B.C.
Author: King Solomon, as a young king
Type of book: A love poem
In a nutshell: Two lovers address each other with an array of emotions.
Characters involved: King Solomon, the Shulammite woman, and the young women of Jerusalem
Claim to fame: The only completely romantic book in the Bible
Place in the Bible: Fifth book of Poetry in the Old Testament

A PG-13 RATING?

It might not always seem like it at first glance, but the Bible is a very practical book. It deals with the issues of everyday life. The Song of Solomon is a good example. This is romantic love at its most syrupy and, sometimes, at its most seductive.

Solomon was the son of a musician and a soldier. His father, David, wrote many of the psalms (which are songs, remember). Solomon came from a creative bloodline. So, out of his love for a beautiful woman, one whom he treasured, came this love poem that is inspired not by Cupid's arrow, but by God Himself.

HOW THE THEOLOGIANS FEEL

As you can imagine, this book of the Bible has created quite a stir through the centuries. For goodness' sake, parts of it are almost pillow talk (young Jewish boys were not allowed to read this book until they were thirteen years old). Because of that, many have been uncomfortable with the interpretation. As the dust settles, most agree that Song of Solomon is a literal love poem about real people.

But most also agree that this book is a great picture of how Christ feels about the Church. The New Testament calls the Church the "bride of Christ." In this way, the desire and passion that the king in this book shows for his bride is akin to the desire and passion that Christ has toward us, His body, His Church. We are valued. We are prized. We are an object of desire. We bring him joy.

SWEET TALK

The next time you're looking for some sweet talk, lift a line from King Solomon:

"You have stolen my heart. . .with one glance of your eyes, with one jewel of your necklace" (Song of Solomon 4:9).

"Set me as a seal upon thine heart, as a seal upon thine arm: for love is strong as death; jealousy is cruel as the grave: the coals thereof are coals of fire, which hath a most vehement flame" (Song of Solomon 8:6 KJV).

"Many waters cannot quench love, neither can the floods drown it: if a man would give all the substance of his house for love, it would utterly be contemned" (Song of Solomon 8:7 KJV).

Isaiah

VITAL STATISTICS

Name: Isaiah, for the prophet who wrote it. His name means
  "salvation of Jehovah."
When written: Somewhere between 700 and 651 B.C.
Author: Isaiah, one of the most famous prophets of Israel
Type of book: A collection of sermons or messages from God called
  prophecies
In a nutshell: Isaiah reminded his readers of two things: that they
  needed to turn away from their sin and back to God AND that a
  Messiah was coming who would forgive and comfort them.
Claim to fame: The New Testament quotes more from Isaiah than any
  other Old Testament prophet.
Place in the Bible: First book of a Major Prophet in the Old Testament

HELD CAPTIVE

Isaiah was written during the time when the Jewish people were in captivity
in Babylonia. They didn't know if they'd ever get home again. They were
discouraged. They were second-class citizens held against their will.

THE FIRST PART OF ISAIAH

The book of Isaiah divides easily into two parts. The first thirty-nine chapters
are about judgment. They refer to events current to Isaiah's day as well as
events that haven't even happened yet today. You'll find that's true of much
of the prophecy in the Bible. There was truth for the people then and there,
but the prophecies also reflected a greater event in the more distant future.

God spoke through Isaiah with compassion and with an in-your-face-
but-because-I-love-you kind of voice.

This part of Isaiah's prophecy is relevant to us today as much as to the
people trapped in Babylonia. We can choose God's way or our own, but only
one will lead us to full lives.

INSPIRED MUSIC

Have you ever heard Handel's *Messiah*? It's a classical choral piece performed often around Christmas. The most well-known song from the collection is the Hallelujah Chorus, which has appeared in everything from church sanctuaries to sitcoms and commercials.

Anyway, if you've heard Handel's *Messiah*, you've heard parts of Isaiah put to music. Check out these scripture lyrics and see if they ring a bell or two. The scriptures listed below are from the King James Version of the Bible, which uses an older style of English. It is the version Handel quoted.

"Every valley shall be exalted, and every mountain and hill shall be made low: and the crooked shall be made straight, and the rough places plain" (Isaiah 40:4). *This describes God's truth revealed in Jesus Christ.*

"And the glory of the LORD shall be revealed, and all flesh shall see it together: for the mouth of the LORD hath spoken it" (Isaiah 40:5). *Jesus is considered the glory of the Lord because He is God revealed to us.*

"Therefore, the LORD himself shall give you a sign; behold, a virgin shall conceive, and bear a son, and shall call his name Immanuel" (Isaiah 7:14). *Did you know the Old Testament actually gave one of the names for Jesus?*

"For unto us a child is born, unto us a son is given: and the government shall be upon his shoulder: and his name shall be called Wonderful, Counselor, The mighty God, The everlasting Father, The Prince of Peace" (Isaiah 9:6). *So many songs have been based on this verse in one version or another.*

"He is despised and rejected of men; a man of sorrows, and acquainted with grief: and we hid as it were our faces from him; he was despised, and we esteemed him not" (Isaiah 53:3). *Jesus was not accepted among His peers. He wasn't recognized for who He was.*

"But he was wounded for our transgressions, he was bruised for our iniquities: the chastisement of our peace was upon him; and with his stripes we are healed" (Isaiah 53:5). *Jesus died for our sins. The stripes refer to the flogging He received before He was killed.*

"All we like sheep have gone astray; we have turned every one to his own way; and the LORD hath laid on him the iniquity of us all" (Isaiah 53:6). *This is the bottom line of the Gospel: Jesus sacrificed Himself for our sin* (that's what iniquity is).

THE SECOND PART

The last twenty-six chapters of Isaiah (40–66) are often called the "Book of Consolation." They speak directly to Jesus' appearance in the New Testament. He was the future Savior, the Messiah. Chapter 53 is one of the most famous and most picturesque prophecies about Jesus' birth, life, and death.

"He was oppressed and afflicted, yet he did not open his mouth; he was led like a lamb to the slaughter, and as a sheep before its shearers is silent, so he did not open his mouth. By oppression and judgment he was taken away. Yet who of his generation protested? For he was cut off from the land of the living; for the transgression of my people he was punished. He was assigned a grave with the wicked, and with the rich in his death, though he had done no violence, nor was any deceit in his mouth" (Isaiah 53:7–9).

No one knew better than Isaiah that when Christ came to earth He would suffer greatly so that we would not have to.

Jeremiah

 VITAL STATISTICS

Name: Jeremiah, for the prophet who wrote it. His name means "Jehovah has appointed."

When written: Between 625 and 575 B.C.

Author: Jeremiah. He's also known as the "Weeping Prophet."

Type of book: A prophecy or message from God

In a nutshell: Jeremiah does his best to talk his people into turning away from their sin.

Claim to fame: Through the centuries since Jeremiah lived and wrote, he has been called the "Weeping Prophet" because he grieved so deeply for the sins of his people.

Place in the Bible: Second book of a Major Prophet in the Old Testament

A FAMOUS METAPHOR

Today in many songs and sermons God is described as a potter and we are described as His clay. That illustration originated with Jeremiah in chapter 18:

*"The word which came to Jeremiah from the L*ORD*, saying: 'Arise and go down to the potter's house, and there I will cause you to hear My words.' Then I went down to the potter's house, and there he was, making something at the wheel. And the vessel that he made of clay was marred in the hand of the potter; so he made it again into another vessel, as it seemed good to the potter to make. Then the word of the L*ORD *came to me, saying: 'O house of Israel, can I not do with you as this potter?' says the L*ORD*. 'Look, as the clay is in the potter's hand, so are you in My hand, O house of Israel!'" (Jeremiah 18:1–6 N*KJV*).*

At the time when Jeremiah wrote this metaphor, God had worked with Israel for years and generations. They continued to turn their backs on God and do life the way THEY wanted, even though it led them to destruction every time. They were like clay on a potter's wheel that He has molded and yet it falls or collapses; it shows its own weakness. This is not very flattering. But the great news is that the potter beats that clay back down so that He can start all over. God continually starts over and over again with Israel.

He does the same with each of us.

WEEPING AND WAILING

Jeremiah had a life that few of us would wish for. He experienced a lot of rejection. He spent most of his whole life and certainly all of his adult life grieving for the mistakes of his fellow citizens. He was a prophet who didn't get a lot of glory.

Jeremiah preached or prophesied mostly in Judah, the southern kingdom of Israel. Like all of Israel, these people had drifted further and further from God's way of doing things. At first Jeremiah's prophecies were warnings such as "You know what ALWAYS happens when you don't follow God. We get weaker and weaker until some other country takes us over."

Later in his ministry, his prophecies resembled something more like "Well, you've made your bed now. You need to get ready to lie in it. You've become too weak with sin and idolatry to fight off anybody. Accept that something bad is going to happen."

Still later he gave up on the current situation and began to prophesy of the eventual salvation. His message was "We have wasted this time as a nation. But there is always eventual hope because God promised a Messiah who will fix this mess we've created."

Sure enough, Jeremiah's people did become captives in Babylonia. Sure enough, Jesus did come to give them, and us, hope. Sure enough, we still create messes for God to fix. Jeremiah still has something to say to us today.

Lamentations

VITAL STATISTICS

Name: Lamentations (This is actually a funeral dirge, thus the name "like a lament.")

When written: Around 600 B.C.

Author: Jeremiah, the same prophet who wrote the prophecies in the book of Jeremiah

Type of book: Sermons or prophecies in the form of songs

In a nutshell: The information in this book can be broken into five different funeral-type songs about the sins of Israel.

Interesting to note: Chapters 1, 2, and 4 are actually acrostics. In their original language (Hebrew), each verse started with a different letter (in order) of the Hebrew alphabet.

Place in the Bible: Third book of a Major Prophet in the Old Testament

NOBODY LIKES ME, EVERYBODY HATES ME, THINK I'LL EAT WORMS
Think of the saddest song you know and you'll be in the right mood for reading Lamentations.

We spend so much of our lives not worrying about sin that it's hard to understand Jeremiah getting so worked up about it. Actually, the people of his day felt the same way. They ridiculed Jeremiah. They rejected his message.

Think about a time when you were small and you did something someone (like a parent or older sibling) was REALLY going to be mad about. You spent some time dreading them coming home and finding out. Then you heard the door opening and you knew what was coming. That period of time between what you did and when they found out—that time when you felt miserable—that is the kind of time Lamentations describes. This book was probably written just as the Jewish people were being taken captive. They were just being caught in the consequences of their actions. We've all been there.

- *"The yoke of my transgressions was bound; they were woven together by His hands, and thrust upon my neck. He made my strength fail; The Lord delivered me into the hands of those whom I am not able to withstand"* (Lamentations 1:14 NKJV).
- *"Why should the living complain when punished for their sins? Let us examine our ways and test them, and let us return to the LORD"* (Lamentations 3:39–40).
- *"The crown is fallen from our head: woe unto us, that we have sinned! For this our heart is faint; for these things our eyes are dim"* (Lamentations 5:16–17 KJV).

But that didn't change the fact that what he said came true. He had told them that if they didn't straighten up, they would lose their land again and... guess what? Sure enough, they were taken captive into Babylonia.

As far as we know, Lamentations was written for the people *while* they were captives. It was pretty good of Jeremiah, when you think about it, to warn the people, get blown off by them, then write them some sad songs when they needed them. (Sad songs say so much, you know.)

Lamentations could have been a told-you-so book. Jeremiah had, indeed, warned the people about the consequences of their sin. But rather than being a told-you-so book, Jeremiah is a book of sadness that his people were (1) separated once again from their land and (2) disobedient to God, which caused them to be separated from their land. When will people ever learn that there are consequences for ignoring God's way of doing things? (Not yet, anyway.)

Ezekiel

VITAL STATISTICS

Name: Ezekiel, for the prophet who wrote it. His name means "the one whom God will strengthen."
When written: Around 550 B.C., to the Jewish people who were in captivity in Babylon
Author: Ezekiel, a Zadokite priest (Say THAT three times fast!)
Type of book: You could call this either a sermon or a prophecy. It includes visions.
In a nutshell: Ezekiel describes God and foretells God's judgment and deliverance.
Place in the Bible: Fourth book of a Major Prophet in the Old Testament

A MAN WITH A VISION

That's Ezekiel. Not just one vision either. Many visions. The book of Ezekiel is a colorful prophecy. It includes judgment and condemnation. It's almost kicking the people while they are down, since he was preaching to them while they were exiled from their homes. The book also includes visions of heaven and hope for the future.

Because Ezekiel is such an imaginative book, it can seem difficult to wade through at times. Just remember this is the writing of a man to whom God is showing spectacular things. Ezekiel is trying to describe his visions of heaven and of heavenly things in human terms. Basically, that is impossible. So he makes a lot of "It was like. . ." kind of statements. In the end we'll all have to wait until we see God to really understand what Ezekiel saw.

Whether we understand Ezekiel's visions or not, we can understand his message that there is reality beyond what we can see and there is hope beyond any difficulty we might face.

WHAT BONES?

One of the most powerful images in Ezekiel is the valley of dry bones. The bones represented Israel, with no hope. God breathed life into the bones to show Ezekiel that there was hope for Israel and that they would one day return to their land. Do you recognize that story? You might recognize it more this way:

'Dem bones, 'Dem bones,
'Dem dry bones,
'Dem bones, 'Dem bones,
'Dem dry bones,
'Dem bones, 'Dem bones,
'Dem dry bones,
now hear the word of the Lord.

The toe bone connected to the ankle bone, the ankle bone connected to the leg bone, the leg bone connected to the hip bone, et cetera, et cetera. . . (See Ezekiel 37:1–14.)

A VISION OF GOD

Sometimes, just as a cute adult thing to do, we ask little kids what they think God looks like. Some responses are hilarious, but none are ever like Ezekiel's view of God. Listen to this:

> *Above the vault over their heads was what looked like a throne of*
> *lapis lazuli, and high above on the throne was a figure like that*
> *of a man. I saw that from what appeared to be his waist up he*
> *looked like glowing metal, as if full of fire, and that from there*
> *down he looked like fire; and brilliant light surrounded him. Like*

the appearance of a rainbow in the clouds on a rainy day, so was
the radiance around him. This was the appearance of the likeness
of the glory of the LORD. When I saw it, I fell facedown.
 EZEKIEL 1:26–28

And listen to his description of the angels around God's throne:

- *"In appearance their form was human. . .each of them had four faces and four wings."*
- *"Their legs were straight; their feet were like those of a calf and gleamed like burnished bronze."*
- *"Under their wings. . .they had human hands."*
- *"Each of the four had the face of a human being. . .the face of a lion. . .the face of an ox. . .also had the face of an eagle."*
- *"The appearance of the living creatures was like burning coals of fire or like torches. . . . The creatures sped back and forth like flashes of lightning."*
- *"I saw a wheel on the ground beside each creature with its four faces. . . . Their rims were high and awesome, and all four rims were full of eyes all around."* (See Ezekiel 1:5–21.)

GOD'S PROMISE

"I will give them an undivided heart and put a new spirit in them; I will remove from them their heart of stone and give them a heart of flesh. Then they will follow my decrees and be careful to keep my laws. They will be my people, and I will be their God" (Ezekiel 11:19–20).

Daniel

DANIEL: THE STORY

The story of Daniel is like a miniseries set in the midst of the exile of the
Jewish people. Daniel was a young adult when his people were taken captive
into Babylonia.

First, the Babylonians tried to feed him rich foods that were taboo for a
young Jewish boy. He opted for vegetables and fruits. Before you knew it, he
had influenced the guards to serve all the boys healthier meals.

Next, he became a servant to the king himself and even interpreted the
king's dreams. Because of this, he was put in charge of all the wise men in
Babylonia.

As you can imagine, this did not sit well with the Babylonian locals. They
set a trap, convincing the king to give an order for everyone, including the
Jewish people, to bow down to an idol. Daniel and his friends refused. You've
probably heard the miraculous story of the three friends being thrown into
the fiery furnace (a form of capital punishment) and not only surviving, but
not even smelling of smoke.

In another attempt to trip up the Jewish people, a decree was sent out that no one could pray to God for thirty days. Daniel, of course, continued to pray. His punishment was to be thrown into a cave with hungry lions. Believe it or not, not one lion touched Daniel.

DIPLOMAT AND NEGOTIATOR

Daniel gives us some awesome examples of the skill of negotiation. At the opening of the book of Daniel, he is a foreigner, a captive in a new land. He is offered food that his faith forbids him to eat. Instead of starving himself, instead of rebelling against his captors, instead of trying to run away, Daniel negotiated. "How about this," he said. "Let us eat the foods we think are best for us and after ten days, you decide who looks healthier."

Through this diplomatic approach Daniel showed how, even in a small way, God's ways are best. From then on he got bigger and bigger opportunities to try out this same strategy and, for him, it worked in his favor every time.

DANIEL: THE PROPHECY

The last half of the book of Daniel is made up of Daniel's prophecies. As far as we know, many of those prophecies have already been fulfilled. Some, though, refer to the same time period as described in the book of Revelation (New Testament), the end of the world.

Hosea, Joel, Amos, Obadiah

 VITAL STATISTICS

Name: Hosea, for the prophet. His name means "salvation."
When written: 715 B.C.
Author: Hosea, a prophet in Israel, the northern kingdom
Type of book: A record or collection of Hosea's prophecies
In a nutshell: An illustration of God's love for His people even though they continued to disregard Him
Place in the Bible: First book of a Minor Prophet in the Old Testament

HOSEA

If anybody knows anything about Hosea, it is usually that he was the prophet who married the prostitute.

Why? Because God told him to.

Why would God tell him to do that? So that his life could be a picture of how much God loved Israel.

Why would God compare Israel to a prostitute? Good question. The answer to this question is the foundation for understanding Hosea. The people of Israel were very much like a prostitute because they were unfaithful to God. God had asked them to worship only Him, no idols, no false gods. Sometimes the people would obey God. Usually those times were when they needed God's help. But as soon as they were doing okay, they forgot their allegiance and began to worship whatever was the popular idol of the day.

This had been going on for years. It had caused them to lose their homes, their battles, their well-being. It was about to cause them to be taken captive to another land, and that's why God asked Hosea for desperate measures. Basically God said, "Marry a call girl and let her despicable actions toward you show these people how they have treated Me."

So that's what Hosea did. He married a prostitute. They had three children together. She constantly broke Hosea's heart by going back to her old life, no matter how much he loved her or how well he treated her.

Maybe some of the Israelites listened. We don't know. They didn't repent of their religious prostitution. They kept right on worshipping other gods until they were destroyed as a nation.

Do we do that same thing? Run to God when we need Him, but give everything else a priority until then? Will we listen to Hosea, even though his people in that day didn't?

VITAL STATISTICS

Name: Joel. In Hebrew this name means "Jehovah is God."
When written: Around 800 B.C.
Author: Joel, one of the early prophets of the southern kingdom, Judah
Type of book: A collection of Joel's prophecies
In a nutshell: This book is Joel's warning to his country, Judah, that God would judge their sin.
Place in the Bible: Second book of a Minor Prophet in the Old Testament

JOEL

In the Old Testament God's judgment for sin came in the form of many things. In the plagues of Egypt, God's judgment came in the form of death and bugs and sickness and weather.

The book of Joel is a red-flag message to the people of Judah that God had just about had enough of their sin. Joel was specific, too. He told his people that their punishment would come in the form of locusts—flying, grasshopper-like bugs that fed off the vegetation of the land.

Punishment by grasshoppers might not sound like much more than an inconvenience to us. We need to understand the culture of that day though. People lived off the land. They farmed; they raised food for their animals. If a huge swarm of locusts came through and destroyed all the vegetation, the people would have nothing. Everyone would eventually starve.

When Joel gave this gloom-and-doom prophecy, everything was going pretty well in Judah. It was difficult for the people to think of hard times when they had plenty to eat. That's why they didn't listen to Joel. That's why they disregarded God's warning that their sin would destroy them.

Joel did give a little good news as well. Like many other prophets, his message included an in-the-future clause. It also applied to the future. He predicted not only Judah's destruction because of their sin, but also Judah's eventual salvation through God's eventual forgiveness.

VITAL STATISTICS

Name: Amos. The Hebrew meaning for this name is "burden" or "burden-bearer."

When written: Around 750 B.C.

Author: Amos, a prophet from Judah (the southern kingdom), who preached to Israel (the northern kingdom)

Type of book: A sermon or prophecy

In a nutshell: God will judge the people of Israel for their idolatry and oppression.

Place in the Bible: Third book by a Minor Prophet in the Old Testament

Key Verse: "Seek good, not evil, that you may live. Then the Lord God Almighty will be with you, just as you say he is" (Amos 5:14).

AMOS

Amos was a fish out of water in a lot of ways. He was from the southern kingdom, but he preached to the northern kingdom. He was a shepherd, but he preached to rich people. His message was somewhat negative, but he was preaching to people who were having a great time.

The meat of Amos's message was that God was not satisfied with the worship of His people in Israel. They were coming to the temple to worship, then making their living by exploiting the poor of their society. They were doing some of the right ceremonial things, but they weren't worshipping God with the way they lived their lives. For this, God, through Amos, condemned them.

One of the ways in which God directed Amos to warn the people was through showing him a plumb line. A plumb line was a string with a weight that showed a workman whether his work was straight. God told Amos that He was holding a plumb line up to Israel to see if their ways were straight or not. They were definitely not making the grade compared to God's plumb line.

Amos's message to us can be much the same as his message to the people of his day. Is our religion empty? Are we exploiting the less fortunate for our own gain, yet calling ourselves religious?

 VITAL STATISTICS

Name: Obadiah. His name means "servant of the Lord" or "worshipper of Jehovah."
When written: Around 850 B.C.
Author: Obadiah
In a nutshell: Obadiah speaks to the enemies of God's people, the Edomites.
Type of book: A prophetic sermon
Place in the Bible: Fourth book by a Minor Prophet in the Old Testament

OBADIAH

Obadiah is unique in that he didn't preach to Israel or Judah. Instead he preached on their behalf to the Edomites.

A little background: Many generations before, the country of Edom originated from a man named Esau (his name later became Edom). Ironically enough, Esau was the twin brother of Jacob (whose name was later changed to Israel). The Israelites and the Edomites were very closely related. But just as Esau and Jacob had their differences (Genesis 25–27), the Israelites and the Edomites had theirs.

Obadiah's prophecy is basically a condemnation of Edom for NOT helping Israel defend itself, and for being a bully to Israel. Obadiah prophesied that the whole nation of Edom would eventually die out. By A.D. 70, they had.

TALK ABOUT A SOAP OPERA

The actual skinny about the Edomites and the Israelites reads like a daytime drama.

Esau (later named Edom) and Jacob (later named Israel) were twin boys who, even in the womb, fought to see who would be the better, the first. Esau was born first, which meant he had the family birthright. This birthright became a conflict that lasted their whole lives.

Esau was a rough outdoorsman. Jacob was just the opposite. One day Esau came in from hunting and he was ravenous. Jacob talked him into trading his birthright for some stew.

The birthright was really nothing without the blessing of their dad (Isaac). When the time came, Jacob dressed up like Esau and went to his dad in disguise to receive Esau's blessing. Isaac was old and almost blind. He mistakenly promised Jacob the bigger part of the inheritance and the leadership role in the family. That might not sound binding today, but in that day it meant everything.

When Esau got back to the house that day, he realized that he had been snookered out of his future as a leader and a rich man. He was left to make his home among foreigners. This is why he ended up in Edom with a huge grudge that he passed along to his people.

Talk about a family feud.

Jonah

 VITAL STATISTICS

Name: Jonah
When written: Around 760 B.C.
Author: Jonah, son of Amittai
Type of book: A story or narrative
In a nutshell: God asked Jonah to prophesy in Nineveh. Jonah ran
the other way but, through a fishy situation, finally obeyed God.
Because he did, a city was saved from destruction and, maybe,
Jonah learned a thing or two.
Claim to fame: The story of Jonah living three days in the belly of a
big fish. (Did you know that the Bible never calls it a whale?)
Place in the Bible: Fifth book by a Minor Prophet in the Old
Testament

A FISHY STORY

The story of Jonah is a classic story of my way versus God's way. God told
Jonah to go to Nineveh and prophesy. (Nineveh was the capital of the biggest
enemy of Jonah's country.) Jonah headed the opposite direction.

He jumped on a boat that ran into a storm, and a bad storm at that. It
was looking like the boat was going to be destroyed when the sailors realized
that God was after something. Jonah fessed up and they (splash!) threw him
overboard. Jonah was swallowed by a big fish and had three days in a dark
belly to contemplate his next move.

Jonah did some praying while he was in the fish, and after those three
days, the fish regurgitated him (yuck!) onto the beach. God once again said
to go to Nineveh; Jonah went.

Thus far this story is pretty familiar. The belly-of-the-fish part is the
famous part. But there is more.

When Jonah got to Nineveh, he preached to the people and they responded
graciously. They repented of their sin and banned evil from their city.

How did Jonah respond? He was disappointed. He had gone to a lot of trouble and come a long way, and here these people had changed their ways and gotten off the hook. Jonah sat himself down and had a big ol' pity party. A plant grew up around him that kept him in the shade. This was good. But the next day, a worm killed the plant and that was bad.

Jonah complained to God. Now, get the picture. Here is a man who spent three days in the belly of a fish and he's complaining because a worm ate a vine. God gave Jonah a little talking-to.

So this is the question: Who is the story of Jonah really about, a wicked town called Nineveh or a thickheaded prophet who needed to learn some lessons?

A VIEW FROM THE BELLY OF A BIG FISH

What would you say if you were in the belly of a fish for three days? This is what Jonah said from his dark, living cave:

"When my soul fainted within me, I remembered the Lord; and my prayer went up to You, into Your holy temple. Those who regard worthless idols forsake their own Mercy. But I will sacrifice to You. With the voice of thanksgiving; I will pay what I have vowed. Salvation is of the Lord" (Jonah 2:7–9 NKJV).

Micah, Nahum, Habakkuk

MICAH

The prophet Micah was unique in that he preached or prophesied to both Israel (called Samaria) and Judah. The other prophets preached to either one or the other. But, like the other prophets, he did speak both of judgment that was surely coming to the Jewish people and of the future victory that would come through Jesus Christ.

Micah called his people back to a heart devotion instead of a faith that just goes through the motions. He foretold their exile to Babylon, which did eventually happen.

Micah closes his writings with a beautiful prayer:

> *Who is a God like You, pardoning iniquity*
> *and passing over the transgression of the remnant of*
> *His heritage? He does not retain His anger forever,*
> *because He delights in mercy.*
> MICAH 7:18 NKJV

This was good news for Israel. It is also good news for us.

WHAT GOD WANTS

"He has shown you, O mortal, what is good. And what does the LORD require of you? To act justly and to love mercy and to walk humbly with your God" (Micah 6:8).

NAHUM

Assyria was Israel and Judah's neighbor to the east, and Assyria was a bully of a neighbor. First Assyria took over Israel. Once that happened, Judah and its capital, Jerusalem, were under constant threat. Nahum directed his prophecy to Assyria and particularly to its capital, Nineveh.

Remember that Nineveh was the town that Jonah prophesied to after the whole big-fish-regurgitated-on-the-beach fiasco. One of the reasons Jonah hadn't wanted to preach to Nineveh was that they were the enemy. That was also why he was less than thrilled when they repented and God did not destroy them.

But Nineveh did not stay in a repented state. They returned to their evil ways and Nahum then confronted them with the news that God would punish evil.

The book of Nahum, like most prophecies, had meaning for Israel in that day, but it also has meaning for us. In many ways Assyria represents the evil that we see in our world today. The message is still true: God will not abide evil forever. He will win over it, if not now, then eventually. That is a comfort when it seems like evil is always one step ahead.

VITAL STATISTICS

Name: Habakkuk. This name means "one who embraces."
When written: About 600 B.C.
Author: Habakkuk, a prophet
Type of book: A prophecy or message given by Habakkuk for God
In a nutshell: God is stronger than the evil in the world.
Claim to fame: Habakkuk 2:4—"The righteous shall live by faith"—is a famous verse that is quoted three times in the New Testament and became an important verse in the Reformation (a big religious movement) of the sixteenth century.
Place in the Bible: Eighth book of a Minor Prophet in the Old Testament

HABAKKUK

Habakkuk asks God the kinds of questions we would often like to ask:

> *How long, LORD, must I call for help,*
> *but you do not listen?*
> *Or cry out to you, 'Violence!'*
> *but you do not save?*
> *Why do you make me look at injustice?*
> *Why do you tolerate wrongdoing?*
> HABAKKUK 1:2–3

Habakkuk was honest enough to ask the hard questions. In fact, that was how his prophecy began. But then Habakkuk also heard God give answers. God said that punishing evil is up to Him alone. He reminds Habakkuk (and us) that evil will not go unpunished in the end.

One of the interesting things about Habakkuk is that he begins with the hard questions and he ends with worship. He accepts God's control over the situation and closes with this prayer:

Though the fig tree does not bud
and there are no grapes on the vines,
though the olive crop fails
and the fields produce no food,
though there are no sheep in the pen
and no cattle in the stalls,
yet I will rejoice in the LORD,
I will be joyful in God my Savior.
HABAKKUK 3:17–18

IN REVIEW

To understand Micah, Nahum, and Habakkuk, remember their situation. Judah has gone back and forth and back and forth with God for generations. They have heard the message over and over again that if they continue to disobey, they will be punished; probably that punishment will come through neighboring enemy nations.

These three prophets are speaking with desperation. Judah's fall was happening quickly. In the minds of these men, they were at their last-ditch attempt to turn their country around, to find some hope amid the doom.

These were the men who were most in touch with the situation because God had given them that kind of insight. They could have run, but they stayed and stood on their soapboxes and gave the message that God had burned on their hearts.

Zephaniah, Haggai, Zechariah, Malachi

ZEPHANIAH

Zephaniah was one of the last prophets to Judah before they were taken captive into Babylonia. His message, though first to Judah, was to all nations. He reminded everyone that God would hold them accountable for their actions. He reminds us still today.

The first section of Zephaniah, which is the section on judgment, is classic among the prophets. You may have heard the term *hellfire and brimstone* used to describe a preacher who is really letting his listeners have it in terms of condemnation. Zephaniah's message started out that way. Then gradually he moved from a place of condemnation to a place of growing hope.

Zephaniah actually followed the pattern of many self-help groups today. First, he knew the people needed to recognize just how much they had messed up. Then he could offer them hope that they weren't alone in their situation. The last portion of Zephaniah even points to the coming of Christ as the greatest hope of salvation.

Name: Haggai. This name means "festival."
When written: 520 B.C. (To be exact, August 29, October 17, and December 18. How do you like that for specifics?)
Author: Haggai the prophet
Type of book: A sermon or prophecy, but his style is often that of a storyteller.
In a nutshell: Put your priority on your relationship with God and the other stuff will work out.
Claim to fame: Haggai is one of the only prophets who did not talk about judgment.
Place in the Bible: Tenth book by a Minor Prophet in the Old Testament

HAGGAI

The book of Haggai is about priorities. Unlike the book of Zephaniah, written before the exile from Judah to Babylon, Haggai was written *after* the exile. The people have returned to Judah but are putting off making God a priority by restoring their place of worship, the temple. Haggai basically confronts them with their procrastination: What are you doing leaving God's house in a mess so you can work on your own?

Haggai's message can seem a little backward to us. After all, we are always hearing that expression, "Charity starts at home." Weren't the people right to work on their own homes first? Well. . .remember two things:

1. It had been at least ten years. It's not like Haggai was telling them to rebuild the temple before they even unpacked their bags. They had established a pattern of not getting around to it.
2. The problem all along with the Jewish people, in fact the reason they lost their homes to begin with, was a lack of priority on worship. God had told them, "Only worship Me." But they hadn't listened. Rebuilding the temple would be a significant step to establishing a new pattern of living.

Haggai also spoke to the people about the future temple. That meant way in the future when Jesus returns to earth and the new heaven and new earth are formed. In this way Haggai, like the other prophets, reminded God's people that life won't always be difficult.

VITAL STATISTICS

Name: Zechariah. This name means "Jehovah—or the Lord—has remembered."

When written: We don't know exactly when these sermons were written down, but Zechariah delivered them on February 15, 519 B.C., and December 7, 518 B.C.

Author: Zechariah, a prophet

Type of book: A sermon or prophecy

In a nutshell: Zechariah reminded the people that God was going to send a Savior.

Claim to fame: This book is the most apocalyptic (visions of the end times) and messianic of all the Minor Prophets.

Place in the Bible: Eleventh book by a Minor Prophet in the Old Testament

ZECHARIAH

The first part of the book of Zechariah relates most closely to the rebuilding of the temple in Jerusalem. Zechariah is writing to motivate the people. "It really is worth it!" was Zechariah's message.

The second part of Zechariah holds more prophecies about Jesus than any other Old Testament prophet.

- Jesus rode into Jerusalem riding on a donkey a week before He died (Zechariah 9:9).
- Judas betrayed Jesus Christ for thirty pieces of silver (Zechariah 11:12).
- Jesus' side was pierced (Zechariah 12:10).
- Jesus' blood cleansed our sin (Zechariah 13:1).

- Jesus had scars in His hands and side (Zechariah 13:6).
- Jesus was arrested and His disciples deserted Him (Zechariah 13:7).

Zechariah also prophesied Jesus' second return to reign on earth (Zechariah 14:4; Revelation 11:15).

VITAL STATISTICS

Name: Malachi. This name means "the messenger of Jehovah [God]."

When written: About 430 B.C.

Author: Malachi, the last prophet until John the Baptist in the New Testament

Type of book: A sermon or prophecy in the form of questions and answers

In a nutshell: Malachi was very honest with his country about their sin. He told them to repent and start following God more closely.

Place in the Bible: Twelfth book by a Minor Prophet in the Old Testament

MALACHI

Malachi is the prophet who connects the Old Testament to the New Testament. He prophesied about John the Baptist and he was the last prophet *until* John the Baptist. While not all the books of the Old Testament are in chronological order, Malachi really is. It was the last book written and it is the last book in the Old Testament.

Malachi reminded the people that they were making a halfhearted attempt at keeping God's law. They brought their sacrifices, but they brought the most damaged of their animals and crops. They were living as if God could not see their hearts and know that they didn't really honor Him.

Malachi also reprimanded the people for the same practice that the Jewish people were guilty of since they came to their land: they continued to marry women who worshipped idols and so the Jewish people began to worship the idols. In Malachi's day, the men were even divorcing their God-fearing wives to marry idol-worshipping wives.

Malachi did foretell Christ's coming as well. He reminded his people that they would be held accountable. He reminds us, too.

Matthew

 VITAL STATISTICS

Name: Matthew, for the writer. His name means "gift of Jehovah."
When Written: Around A.D. 60
Author: Matthew, who was also called Levi. He was one of the twelve disciples and a tax collector.
Type of book: A biographical narrative; a collection of true stories about one person: Jesus
In a nutshell: Matthew wrote this biography of Jesus to prove that Jesus was the Messiah. The book is addressed primarily to the Jewish people.
Claim to fame: Matthew uses more quotes from the Old Testament than any other New Testament book.
Place in the Bible: First Gospel in the New Testament

THE BOOK

The book of Matthew is the first of four Gospels, or versions of the story of Christ. Each of the Gospels has a different slant, a different perspective. They tell the stories in a different order or with different details. Each of the writers gives a true but different viewpoint on Jesus' life.

This was Matthew's slant: Jesus is the promised Messiah. Matthew included more Old Testament prophecies than any other writer. He traced Jesus' genealogy back to Abraham, who is the father of the Jewish people. Matthew established Jesus' role as the one whom the Jewish people had been waiting for.

THE PROBLEM

Unfortunately, that was pretty difficult for the Jewish people to swallow. Throughout the Old Testament, they had heard the promise of the Messiah. Each time the Jewish people were oppressed (even if it was a consequence of their own sin), they comforted themselves by remembering the promise of the Messiah. The problem was, they thought the Messiah was going to be a political and military ruler who would destroy their enemies with a single blast. That was not the kind of messiah Jesus was, at least not this first time around.

As Matthew revealed, Jesus came to die for our sins, not beat up our enemies. He came to show us another way of *living*, not winning.

This is why the religious leaders of the day didn't get it. Here was Jesus. They knew His parents. They had been to His hometown. He didn't look like anything special to them. And He was claiming to be God?! They just couldn't go for that. Add to that the fact that Jesus confronted them on a regular basis about their own hypocrisy, and they were basically out to get Him.

So after all the dust had settled, after Jesus had lived before Matthew's eyes and worked miracles and died and come back to life and then gone back to heaven—then Matthew sat down to set the record straight. He methodically recorded the events and the teachings of Jesus' life so that any reader would know, without a doubt, that Jesus was the Messiah.

A NEW KINGDOM

Jesus had come to establish a new kingdom all right—it just wasn't the kingdom of Israel. It was a new kingdom in people's hearts. That was difficult for the Jewish people of that day to understand, so many rejected Jesus and convinced themselves that they must be looking for someone else.

Matthew closed his version of Jesus' life with a famous statement that we now call the "Great Commission."

*"Therefore go and make disciples of all nations, baptizing them
in the name of the Father and of the Son and of the Holy Spirit,
and teaching them to obey everything I have commanded you.
And surely I am with you always, to the very end of the age."*
MATTHEW 28:19–20

In other words, Jesus came to establish the kingdom of heaven in the hearts of people. Now He wants us to do our part to do the same.

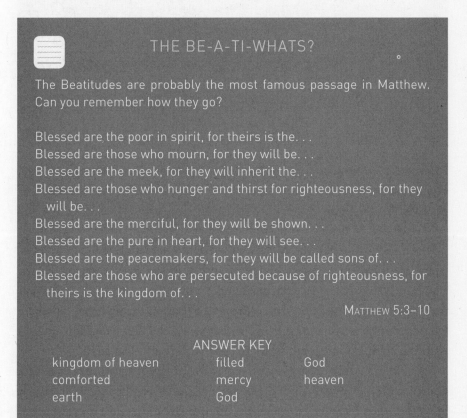

THE BE-A-TI-WHATS?

The Beatitudes are probably the most famous passage in Matthew. Can you remember how they go?

Blessed are the poor in spirit, for theirs is the. . .
Blessed are those who mourn, for they will be. . .
Blessed are the meek, for they will inherit the. . .
Blessed are those who hunger and thirst for righteousness, for they will be. . .
Blessed are the merciful, for they will be shown. . .
Blessed are the pure in heart, for they will see. . .
Blessed are the peacemakers, for they will be called sons of. . .
Blessed are those who are persecuted because of righteousness, for theirs is the kingdom of. . .

MATTHEW 5:3–10

ANSWER KEY

kingdom of heaven	filled	God
comforted	mercy	heaven
earth	God	

Mark

VITAL STATISTICS

Name: Mark
When Written: Around A.D. 60
Author: John Mark, a friend of Peter who went with Paul on his first missionary journey
Type of book: A narrative; like a biography of the life of Jesus Christ
In a nutshell: Mark wrote his story for Romans rather than Jewish people. He revealed Christ through His miraculous works.
Claim to fame: Mark is the shortest of the Gospels and the most active. He writes more about what Jesus did than what Jesus said.
Place in the Bible: Second Gospel in the New Testament

LIGHTS, ACTION!

Mark was a writer who loved action verbs. He wrote about what Christ *did*, His miracles especially. His Gospel is the shortest of all four Gospels. It is the most "to the point."

Mark and Matthew wrote from different standpoints. Matthew focused on the messiahship of Jesus. Mark focused on the servant leadership of Jesus. Matthew spoke to a Jewish audience and built his case based on Jewish tradition. Mark spoke to a Roman audience and focused on Jesus' compassion for all humanity. Mark told three miracles of Jesus in the first chapter where Matthew only had one miracle in the first seven chapters. Matthew opened with the birth of Christ, but Mark opened with Jesus as an adult.

Mark represented Jesus as a servant. He displayed Jesus' miracles as acts of compassion. Almost half of the book of Mark covers the last eight days of Jesus' life when He gave Himself away for our salvation—His greatest act of servanthood.

MARK'S SOURCES

Though Mark was not a disciple of Jesus, he was connected to Jesus in several ways. The disciples met at his mother's home. He was very close to the disciple Peter. His cousin was Barnabas, a colleague of the apostle Paul. Mark even traveled with Paul and Barnabas for a time on one of their missionary journeys.

Since Mark was a "cut-to-the-chase" kind of guy, he had some real bottom-line verses that put a lot of truth in a little space for us to digest:

> *Then [Jesus] called the crowd to him along with his disciples*
> *and said: "Whoever wants to be my disciple must deny*
> *themselves and take up their cross and follow me. For whoever*
> *wants to save their life will lose it, but whoever loses their*
> *life for me and for the gospel will save it. What good is it for*
> *someone to gain the whole world, yet forfeit their soul?"*
> MARK 8:34–36

> *"For even the Son of Man did not come to be served, but to*
> *serve, and to give his life as a ransom for many."*
> MARK 10:45

THE LAST WEEK OF JESUS' MINISTRY

Of the sixteen chapters in Mark, the last seven (almost half!) cover the last week of Christ's life. Chapter 11 begins with Jesus' entry into Jerusalem. This event was perhaps the most misunderstood event of Christ's adult ministry. The people were looking for a king, a political military leader who could rid them of their oppression. When they welcomed Jesus that day into the city, they thought they were welcoming that kind of leader.

But Jesus was coming to Jerusalem to die for the sins of the world, not to become a national leader for a small nation.

During that last week, Mark records several significant events to help us understand Jesus' mission. He records conversations that Jesus had with the religious leaders of the day, trying to clarify for them that He was there as the Son of God. But all they could ask Him about were taxes and tricky questions that might prove their superiority.

Mark records for us the story you've probably heard about the widow who gives her small offering—two coins. But Jesus used her offering to teach the disciples because she gave all that she had.

MARK'S CLOSING REMARKS

Mark records for us with his usual brevity the last supper that Jesus shared with His disciples and then His trial, death, and subsequent burial.

Mark closes his Gospel with the resurrection of Christ, the empty tomb, and the angel explaining to the women (and to the world through Mark) that Jesus was, indeed, dead but had come back to life and was once again about God's business. This is the very thing Mark had set out to reveal all along.

Luke

 VITAL STATISTICS

Name: Luke
When written: Around A.D. 60
Author: Luke, a doctor who was not a Jew. He also wrote Acts.
Type of book: A biographical narrative: the true stories of Jesus' life
In a nutshell: Jesus was God, but He was also completely human and so He has walked our road.
Place in the Bible: Third Gospel in the New Testament
Key verse: *"The Son of Man came to seek and to save the lost"* (Luke 19:10).

THE GOOD DOCTOR

Matthew, the disciple and former tax collector, wrote to convince the Jewish people that Jesus was the promised Messiah. Mark, the missionary sidekick, wrote to convince the Romans that Jesus was a servant and a savior. Luke, the doctor, writes to convince his Greek friend, Theophilus, that Jesus was God, but also fully and completely human.

Since I myself have studied everything carefully from the beginning, most excellent Theophilus, it seemed good for me to write it out for you. I arranged it in order to help you know that what you have been taught is true.

LUKE 1:3–4 NCV

Matthew opens with a genealogy because that's what would matter to his audience. Mark opens with Jesus' adult ministry because that's what would matter to his audience. Luke opens with a whole lot of celebration. Maybe that's what Theophilus needed to hear. Maybe it's what we need to hear as well.

There's a lot of joy in the opening of Luke. Zechariah, an old priest, is happy that his wife will finally bear a child. Mary the mother of Jesus is happy that God has chosen to use her. Elizabeth, Zechariah's wife, is happy that she and Mary are pregnant with boys who will make a difference for God. Zechariah is happy when he finally gets his voice back after the birth of his son, John.

The angels were happy when they told the shepherds that Jesus was finally born. The shepherds were happy enough to travel into the city and greet this baby-king.

When Mary and Joseph take Jesus to the temple to dedicate their baby, they meet two older people, Anna and Simeon, who recognize that Jesus isn't just *any* baby, and they celebrate right then and there.

LUKE'S STRATEGY

Because Luke was writing from the perspective of the wonder of Jesus' humanity, he included some interesting facts that the other Gospel writers didn't include. He gave insights into Christ's childhood and into His dealings with people that show He had compassion. Luke's writings also show us the side of Christ that wasn't too high and mighty to get down and dirty when ministry demanded it.

Luke reveals to us Jesus' friendships. He mentions more women than any other Gospel. He reveals to us that Jesus really was God come to earth to walk many hard miles in our sandals. Luke reveals to us a Jesus who ultimately died so that we could find forgiveness.

WON'T YOU BE MY NEIGHBOR?

Luke tells us that a man once asked Jesus how to get eternal life, to which Jesus said, "Well, what do *you* think?" (Jesus often adopted this strategy, a question for a question.)

The man replied, "To love God with everything you've got and to love your neighbor as yourself." When Jesus agreed with him that this was certainly the way to eternal life, the man became a little more slippery. "And who is my neighbor?"

From that conversation comes one of the most famous stories in the Bible. It is a story that people who have never even read the Bible refer to in everyday conversation when they call someone a "Good Samaritan."

> Then Jesus answered and said: "A certain man went down from Jerusalem to Jericho, and fell among thieves, who stripped him of his clothing, wounded him, and departed, leaving him half dead. Now by chance a certain priest came down that road. And when he saw him, he passed by on the other side. Likewise a Levite, when he arrived at the place, came and looked, and passed by on the other side. But a certain Samaritan, as he journeyed, came where he was. And when he saw him, he had compassion. So he went to him and bandaged his wounds, pouring on oil and wine; and he set him on his own animal, brought him to an inn, and took care of him. On the next day, when he departed, he took out two denarii, gave them to the innkeeper, and said to him, 'Take care of him; and whatever more you spend, when I come again, I will repay you.'" (Luke 10:30–35 NKJV)

After Jesus told this little story, He asked the man, "Which one was the neighbor?" Of course the man replied, "The one who helped." In so many words, Jesus charged him, "You go be a neighbor like *that*."

Jesus never lets us off the hook when it comes to being good people.

Here are some stories that Luke includes that none of the other writers included. These stories give us insight into Jesus' everyday life.

Jesus visits two friends, Mary and Martha, in their home. Martha is an organizer and is running around breathless. Mary is an admirer and is sitting at Jesus' feet. When Martha complains, Jesus affirms Mary's choice to just be with Him (Luke 10:38–42).

One day Jesus was teaching His disciples within earshot of the Pharisees. The Pharisees were religious leaders who had (more often than not) made a business of their piety. They loved money and they loved looking righteous. It's interesting that Jesus chose to tell several stories about people who invested in the wrong kinds of things, or just didn't invest at all. Then when their boss, or their maker, held them accountable, they didn't have much to say for their lives. Jesus didn't win any points with the Pharisees that day (Luke 16:1–17:10).

Ten lepers came to Jesus to be healed. Jesus healed them and sent them to the priest to be proclaimed well. Out of the ten, only one came back to express his gratitude. Jesus asked him, with perhaps a twinkle in His eye, something like: "Now weren't there ten of you? Where are your buddies?" (Luke 17:11–19).

Jesus tells two parables about prayer. In the first, a widow comes to a judge to ask for a judgment against her enemy. She is a woman and she is a widow, so she is not high on the power scale. But because of her perseverance, the judge finally grants her request. In the second, two men pray at the temple. One is proud and prays to be seen by others. One is humble and prays to be forgiven by God. Jesus explains to His listeners that the humble man is the one God hears (Luke 18:1–14).

LUKE AND CHARLIE BROWN

If you've ever watched the Charlie Brown Christmas special, you've heard a passage from Luke. Imagine Linus standing in the spotlight as you read this account of Christ's birth.

And it came to pass in those days, that there went out a decree from Caesar Augustus, that all the world should be taxed. (And this taxing was first made when Cyrenius was governor of Syria.) And all went to be taxed, every one into his own city. And Joseph also went up from Galilee, out of the city of Nazareth, into Judaea, unto the city of David, which is called Bethlehem; (because he was of the house and lineage of David:) to be taxed with Mary his espoused wife, being great with child. And so it was, that, while they were there, the days were accomplished that she should be delivered. And she brought forth her firstborn son, and wrapped him in swaddling clothes, and laid him in a manger; because there was no room for them in the inn. And there were in the same country shepherds abiding in the field, keeping watch over their flock by night. And, lo, the angel of the Lord came upon them, and the glory of the Lord shone round about them: and they were sore afraid. And the angel said unto them, Fear not: for, behold, I bring you good tidings of great joy, which shall be to all people. For unto you is born this day in the city of David a Saviour, which is Christ the Lord. And this shall be a sign unto you; Ye shall find the babe wrapped in swaddling clothes, lying in a manger. And suddenly there was with the angel a multitude of the heavenly host praising God, and saying, Glory to God in the highest, and on earth peace, good will toward men. (Luke 2:1–14 KJV)

John

VITAL STATISTICS

Name: John, for the disciple who wrote it

When written: Around A.D. 90

Author: John the disciple. He was called a "Son of Thunder." (He also wrote 1, 2, and 3 John and Revelation.)

Type of book: Gospel narrative: tells the story of the events and teaching of the life of Jesus Christ. This book is more of a profile of Jesus than a biography. John introduces us to Jesus, rather than just the events of His life.

In a nutshell: John wrote his book to prove without a doubt that Jesus is the Son of God.

Claim to fame: John starts his Gospel by telling us that Jesus was present at the creation of the world.

Place in the Bible: Fourth Gospel in the New Testament

Key verse: *"For God so loved the world, that he gave his only begotten Son, that whosoever believeth in him should not perish, but have everlasting life" (John 3:16 KJV).*

JOHN'S GOSPEL

John wrote his Gospel after Matthew, Mark, and Luke were already written. These three Gospels were very much alike. The book of John added some variety.

Matthew focused on Christ's messiahship, which was a very Jewish issue. Mark focused on Jesus as a servant. Luke focused on Christ's humanity, even though He was deity. John focused on Jesus as the Son of God, His deity even though He was human.

Matthew opened with a genealogy. Mark opened with the beginning of Jesus' adult ministry. Luke opened with the celebration of Jesus' birth. John opens with a symbolic, almost poetic, definitely philosophic introduction of Jesus at the very creation of the world.

In the beginning was the Word, and the Word was with God,
and the Word was God. He was with God in the beginning.
Through him all things were made; without him nothing
was made that has been made. In him was life,
and that life was the light of all mankind. . . .
The Word became flesh and made his dwelling among us.
We have seen his glory, the glory of the One and Only Son,
who came from the Father, full of grace and truth.

JOHN 1:1–4, 14

John establishes Jesus' deity by revealing that He created the very world in which we live.

THE INCARNATION

When Jesus became man, took on a human body, it is called the "incarnation" (you've probably heard of reincarnation more than just incarnation). It was and is still a mystery. How can someone be fully God and fully person? It takes faith to believe.

If God wasn't fully human, His death for our sins wouldn't mean the same thing. If He wasn't fully God, His death for our sins wouldn't mean anything. One person can't just decide to take a punishment for the whole world. It takes God, the Creator of the universe, to decide that.

ONLY IN JOHN

Here are some stories from the life of Jesus that you can only find in the Gospel of John.

- John is the only Gospel that places Jesus' first miracle at a wedding where they ran out of wine. At the request of His mother, Jesus changed some water into wine so the host wouldn't be embarrassed (John 2:1–11).
- From the beginning of His ministry, Jesus confronted the men who made the temple into a marketplace (John 2:12–25).

- Nicodemus came to Jesus at night to find out if He was for real. It was during Jesus' conversation with this man that He said the words we now know as John 3:16 (John 3:1–21).
- You may have heard the story that is often called "Jesus and the Woman at the Well." Besides being a woman (in a culture that devalued women), this woman was a Samaritan (with whom the Jewish people had a major racial conflict). Her conversation with Jesus reveals His lack of concern for status and His love for humans in general (John 4:1–42).
- In an amazing account, Jesus is confronted by the religious leaders with a woman who was caught in adultery (at that time punishable by death). Rather than condemn her, Jesus confronted the sin in the lives of the accusers (John 8:1–11).
- Jesus raised Lazarus, His friend, from the dead, just by calling his name (John 11:1–44).

Acts

 VITAL STATISTICS

Name: Acts or Acts of the Apostles or Acts of the Holy Spirit
When written: Around A.D. 65
Author: Luke, who also wrote the Gospel of Luke. He was a physician.
Type of book: A historical narrative: true stories described chronologically
In a nutshell: The early church received the Holy Spirit and then organized to reach the world for Christ.
Place in the Bible: The only book of History in the New Testament
Key verse: *"But you will receive power when the Holy Spirit comes on you; and you will be my witnesses in Jerusalem, and in all Judea and Samaria, and to the ends of the earth" (Acts 1:8).*

WALKING ACROSS ACTS

The book of Acts is like a bridge between the Gospels and the Epistles (or letters) of the New Testament. The Gospels contain the story of Jesus' life and ministry. The Epistles contain encouragement and training for the early church. The book of Acts reveals how the Church got organized from a group of bewildered disciples to the one true world religion.

PENTECOST

Just after Jesus had returned to heaven (this is after His death and resurrection), the Jewish people were scheduled to celebrate an annual feast called Pentecost. As they gathered together, an unexpected and wonderful thing happened. The Holy Spirit came.

> *"All this I have spoken while still with you. But the Advocate,*
> *the Holy Spirit, whom the Father will send in my name,*
> *will teach you all things and will remind you of*
> *everything I have said to you."*
> JOHN 14:25–26

This event happened miraculously with quite a bit of fanfare:

> *When the Day of Pentecost had fully come, they were all with*
> *one accord in one place. And suddenly there came a sound from*
> *heaven, as of a rushing mighty wind, and it filled the whole*
> *house where they were sitting. Then there appeared to them*
> *divided tongues, as of fire, and one sat upon each of them. And*
> *they were all filled with the Holy Spirit and began to speak*
> *with other tongues, as the Spirit gave them utterance. And*
> *there were dwelling in Jerusalem Jews, devout men, from*
> *every nation under heaven. And when this sound occurred, the*
> *multitude came together, and were confused, because everyone*
> *heard them speak in his own language. Then they were all*

amazed and marveled, saying to one another, "Look, are not all these who speak Galileans? And how is it that we hear, each in our own language in which we were born?"

ACTS 2:1–8 NKJV

This was the beginning of the early Church. At this point those who believed in Jesus' resurrection began to get organized. They began to determine specific ministry roles. They began to share their money and possessions with those who didn't have any. They began to organize to go out and share the news of Jesus' forgiveness through His death. Everything was fresh and new. The rules had all changed. The Church was changing with them.

FIRSTS OF ACTS

First martyr: Stephen, a man of integrity who believed with all his heart that Jesus was the Son of God. Because he would not let go of this belief, the religious leaders stoned him to death (Acts 7:54–60).

First use of the term *Christians*: At Antioch this is what the believers were called (Acts 11:26). We are so used to the word *Christians* at this point in history that it's difficult to imagine a time when it wasn't used. Before Christ's ministry, though, people were either Jewish people or Greeks or Romans. Their faith was determined by their nationality. All of a sudden, then, a person could follow Christ's teaching, no matter what his nationality was. So how could you identify these people? There could be Christian Jews and Christian Greeks. It was like a whole new hybrid was formed and needed a name.

First apostle who never saw Jesus: Saul was converted when Jesus' Spirit struck him blind on the road to Tarsus. He eventually regained his sight and became a great missionary (Acts 9:1–22). Even though he was never a part of Jesus' earthly ministry, Paul encountered Christ and so called himself an "apostle."

THE EARLY CHURCH

The early believers did the only thing they knew to do: they loved one another and shared the news of Christ's forgiveness.

One of the main leaders of the early Church was, surprisingly, the disciple Peter. This is the guy who, during Jesus' trial, denied he even knew Christ. Yet after Pentecost Peter became a mainstay of early Christian leadership.

The same religious leaders who had opposed Jesus when He was on earth, opposed the early Church. They persecuted the apostles.

MISSION TRIPS

Once the Church had its main base organized, it was time to spread out. Acts records several "missionary journeys" in which Paul and others spread the good news that Christ had risen from the dead and could forgive sin once and for all.

Missionary Journey #1

Paul and Barnabas made this journey together. Barnabas was one of the Christians who was brave enough to befriend Paul soon after his conversion. They traveled together from Antioch to Cyprus and then Galatia. The New Testament book Galatians was written by Paul back to the churches he had helped on this journey.

Missionary Journey #2

Paul took a team of missionaries with him on this second journey: Silas, Luke, and Timothy. They visited Philippi, Thessalonica, Berea, Corinth, and Athens. You may recognize several books of the Bible that were written back to these churches: Philippians, 1 and 2 Thessalonians, and 1 and 2 Corinthians.

Missionary Journey #3

Paul went to Ephesus (he later wrote a letter to the churches there: Ephesians) for a lengthy stay, then traveled back through Greece and to Jerusalem.

REMEMBER THE CONTEXT

By the time the three missionary journeys were completed, Christianity was raising quite a ruckus. The message and life of Jesus Christ had upset everyone from Jewish religious leaders to the Roman emperors (who saw themselves as gods).

After the third missionary journey, Paul was put in jail. What the government had in mind was to squelch Paul's influence.

So what did they do? They transported him to Rome, the center of all commerce and communication. They placed him under house arrest (which allowed him visitors), and he basically set up a base of operations right under their noses. He wrote many of the letters we know as the Epistles of the New Testament and encouraged Christians everywhere.

Eventually Paul was killed for his faith, but until then he didn't miss an opportunity to share the news that had really turned the world on its ear: Jesus Christ was the Son of God and gave Himself for our sins.

THE JEW-VERSUS-GENTILE REVOLUTION

If you remember anything about the Old Testament, you should remember that most of it is about the history of the Jewish nation. Their whole story came out of a promise God made to a man named Abraham. Their prophets constantly promised them a messiah, a deliverer.

With such a rich history, it isn't surprising that the Jewish people who accepted Christ's deity didn't really want to share Him with the non-Jewish world. He was their promised Messiah, after all. If anyone wanted to accept Christ's substitution for their sin, let them be circumcised and become a Jew!

During Acts, God was consistently breaking down these barriers. No one needed to become a Jew. Jesus had completed what the Jewish law required. Now it was time for everyone to have access to God just because of their faith in Christ.

We take for granted this kind of thinking today: God's love for everyone. But at that time, it was a major shift in thought and probably a scary one for these people who suffered so much to tell others about Jesus.

It truly was a revolution.

Romans

VITAL STATISTICS

Name: Romans, for the people the book was written to
When written: Around A.D. 60
Author: Paul the apostle
Type of book: A letter of explanation about the Christian life
In a nutshell: You are saved by God's grace, not by the good things you do.
Claim to fame: This book is so filled with a clear understanding of what it means to be a Christian that it is often considered the basic text of Christianity.
Place in the Bible: First letter (Epistle) in the New Testament
Key verse: *"You see, at just the right time, when we were still powerless, Christ died for the ungodly. Very rarely will anyone die for a righteous person, though for a good person someone might possibly dare to die. But God demonstrates his own love for us in this: While we were still sinners, Christ died for us"* (Romans 5:6–8).

WHAT IT ALL MEANS

Paul wrote to the Romans in preparation for his trip there. He wanted them to know as much as possible up front so that when he came they could spend their time digging deeper into their understanding of what Jesus Christ's life and death meant.

While the book of Romans isn't a stuffy book, it *is* a doctrinal book. It is a book that lays out the logic of Christianity:

- We all sin and need to be right with God.
- We are not clean before God no matter how many good things we try to do.

- Jesus came as a sacrifice for our sin; He took our punishment.
- Because He did, we can be alive spiritually instead of dead in sin.
- Before we can be alive spiritually, we have to believe that only through Christ's death and resurrection can we have this new life. It is an act of faith.
- God gives us this new life only through this act of faith. We can't earn it. We can't buy it.

THE REFORMATION

You might remember a period of history called the Reformation. This religious movement was begun by Martin Luther. (Not Martin Luther King Jr.; that was a different period of history.) Martin Luther didn't mean to start the Reformation. He didn't wake up one day and say, "Well, today is a good

ROMANS ROAD

Many people use the book of Romans to explain how to become a Christian. They use some of Paul's logic to walk through an understanding of Christianity, and they call it the Romans Road. Here are some of the biggest road signs on the Romans Road:

"There is none righteous, not even one" (Romans 3:10 NASB).

"For all have sinned and fall short of the glory of God" (Romans 3:23 NASB).

"The wages of sin is death, but the gift of God is eternal life in Christ Jesus our Lord" (Romans 6:23).

"If you declare with your mouth, 'Jesus is Lord,' and believe in your heart that God raised him from the dead, you will be saved. For it is with your heart that you believe and are justified, and it is with your mouth that you profess your faith and are saved" (Romans 10:9–10).

"Everyone who calls on the name of the Lord will be saved" (Romans 10:13).

day for a revolution."

Actually all he did was read the book of Romans. During Martin Luther's day, people worked harder and harder to try to make themselves right before God. Many of the church leadership exploited this desire to "work your way to heaven." When Martin Luther read the book of Romans, he realized, "It's not about being good enough or working hard enough. It's about God's grace. He gave us a gift in Christ's death, and He just asks that we believe that He did it."

Martin Luther started preaching that message, and it started a revolution of thought that we now call the Reformation. It changed the way the world did church, and things have never been the same.

ONE OF THE MOST FAMOUS VERSES IN ROMANS

"And we know that in all things God works for the good of those who love him, who have been called according to his purpose" (Romans 8:28).

1 Corinthians

 VITAL STATISTICS

Name: 1 Corinthians
When written: Around A.D. 50
Author: Paul the apostle. He had visited this church on his second missionary journey.
Type of book: A letter of instruction
In a nutshell: Keep your lives pure and full of love.
Claim to fame: Chapter 13 is a chapter on love. It is often quoted in weddings.
Place in the Bible: Second letter (Epistle) in the New Testament

1 CORINTHIANS

Paul had helped start the church at Corinth. It was a sin-filled city and badly needed a church. It was difficult, though, for the church to not get sucked back into the sin around them.

Paul wrote 1 Corinthians as a response to a letter that he received from the Christians there. They let him know that things were NOT going as planned. Husbands and wives were not being faithful. People in the church were not getting along. Things were getting pretty messy.

So Paul wrote back. His response is what we know as 1 Corinthians.

THE ISSUES AT HAND

There are several passages in 1 Corinthians that have been so relevant to the church in every generation that if you hear enough sermons, you are going to hear something from these passages. They are the passages that show us that the issues we face in church today are not much different than the issues the early Church faced. Cultures change, but human nature is human nature.

1. Division and Disagreements

"What I mean is this: One of you says, 'I follow Paul'; another, 'I follow Apollos'; another, 'I follow Cephas'; still another, 'I follow Christ.' Is Christ divided? Was Paul crucified for you? Were you baptized in the name of Paul?" (1 Corinthians 1:12–13).

Instead of following Jesus, the Corinthians were doing what is still very natural for humans to do. They were following men, usually the man who introduced them to the faith. Paul directed their faith back to Jesus Christ and only Him.

WHAT THE WORLD NEEDS NOW IS LOVE

First Corinthians 13 gives us a description of true love.

"Love is patient, love is kind. It does not envy, it does not boast, it is not proud. It is not rude, it is not self-seeking, it is not easily angered, it keeps no record of wrongs. Love does not delight in evil but rejoices with the truth. It always protects, always trusts, always hopes, always perseveres. Love never fails" (1 Corinthians 13:4–8).

If this is how God wants us to love, how do we measure up?

2. Right and Wrong

The Corinthian church was surrounded by a culture much like our own in which sexual purity (abstinence outside of marriage) was not "in." It's easy for a church to be influenced by the culture around it. Paul reminded this church to follow the teachings of Christ, even if it meant giving up destructive behaviors that they enjoyed. He reminded them to hold one another accountable.

3. Spiritual Gifts

In chapter 12 of 1 Corinthians, Paul explained the concept of spiritual gifts. He said that each person has a gift through the Holy Spirit. The purpose of these gifts is to help the Church—"for the common good," is how he puts it.

Our gifts don't do anyone any good if we are comparing and bickering and fighting over them. No gifts are better than others. God gives us the gift that is best for us. Did you realize that you have a gift, a gift from God even? God wants you to use that gift to make the Church better.

2 Corinthians

 VITAL STATISTICS

Name: 2 Corinthians
When written: Around A.D. 50
Author: Paul the apostle.
Type of book: A letter of instruction
In a nutshell: Paul establishes his credibility as an apostle of Christ.
Place in the Bible: Third letter (Epistle) in the New Testament
Key verse: *"Therefore, if anyone is in Christ, he is a new creation; old things have passed away; behold, all things have become new"* (2 Corinthians 5:17 NKJV).

THE SITUATION

Have you ever tried to work out a conflict long distance? It's difficult, isn't it? All the he-saids, she-saids seem impossible to control through phone calls or e-mail or letters.

That's the kind of battle Paul was trying to deal with when he wrote 2 Corinthians. He had helped start the church at Corinth on one of his missionary journeys. After leaving, though, he heard about some shaky situations there. That caused him to write 1 Corinthians. It was a firm and confrontational letter.

After that things seemed to calm down. Then Paul started hearing that people in the church were criticizing him and actually trying to discredit him. He wrote them again. This time his letter was very personal and less confrontational. This time he let them know more of who he was, rather than just what he thought. He opened his heart a bit and let them know of his love and his commitment to them.

! PAUL'S THORN IN THE FLESH

You might have heard someone talk about their "thorn in the flesh." They usually mean something that is an irritation, but they can't get rid of it so they'll just have to live with it.

That phrase actually finds its origin in 2 Corinthians. *"To keep me from becoming conceited because of these surpassingly great revelations, I was given a thorn in my flesh, a messenger of Satan, to torment me. Three times I pleaded with the Lord to take it away from me. But he said to me, 'My grace is sufficient for you, for my power is made perfect in weakness.' Therefore I will boast all the more gladly about my weaknesses, so that Christ's power may rest on me"* (2 Corinthians 12:7–9).

A lot of people have tried to guess what Paul's thorn in the flesh was. Because of some statements he makes in other letters, some think he had a problem with his eyesight. No one knows for sure, though. All that we know is that sometimes the things that seem to hold us back are the things that God uses to shine through us and to draw us closer to Him.

STANDING UP FOR HIMSELF

Because there were people discrediting him, Paul stood up for himself to the Corinthians. He traced his path in ministry. He established the experiences that had allowed him to be used by God. He walked that thin line between bragging and just telling it like it is.

Paul knew that in order to continue ministering to the church at Corinth he needed to stand up to his detractors. That's exactly what he did in 2 Corinthians.

Galatians

VITAL STATISTICS

Name: Galatians, because it was written to the people who lived in Galatia

When written: Around A.D. 50

Author: Paul the apostle

Kind of book: A letter of instruction and explanation

In a nutshell: Paul was writing to disagree with some people called Judaizers, whose teachings were keeping the Galatian Christians from being free in Christ.

Place in the Bible: Fourth letter (Epistle) in the New Testament

Key verses: *"It is for freedom that Christ has set us free. Stand firm, then, and do not let yourselves be burdened again by a yoke of slavery"* (Galatians 5:1).

"You, my brothers and sisters, were called to be free. But do not use your freedom to indulge the flesh; rather, serve one another humbly in love" (Galatians 5:13).

FREEDOM VERSUS CHAINS

When Paul had visited Galatia, he had explained Christianity to people who were not Jewish people. After he left, though, these new Christians were influenced by people called "Judaizers." The Judaizers believed that anyone who wanted to be a Christian should become a Jew, or at least observe Jewish customs, like circumcision and yearly feasts.

The problem was not the Jewish customs so much as the attitude that a person couldn't be a Christian unless they observed these customs, as if salvation was something that could be earned.

> *I am astonished that you are so quickly deserting the one who*
> *called you to live in the grace of Christ and are turning to a*
> *different gospel—which is really no gospel at all.*
> GALATIANS 1:6–7

It was because of the influence of the Judaizers that Paul wrote the book of Galatians. He wrote to emphasize that the grace of God is free, absolutely free. There is nothing anyone can do to deserve it or earn it. If we think we can, then we lock ourselves up in chains of obedience to something that really doesn't matter.

TO PAY OR NOT TO PAY

Sometimes it's easier to feel like we can earn God's love and acceptance. After all, if He gives it to us for free, we don't feel like we've paid our dues. No matter what feels good to us, though, we can never be good enough or perfect enough to really deserve God's approval. Getting it for free, out of His grace, is the only way we're ever going to get it.

> *You who are trying to be justified by law have been alienated*
> *from Christ; you have fallen away from grace.*
> GALATIANS 5:4

GALATIANS, THE COUSIN TO ROMANS

In many ways Galatians has the same message as Romans. It is shorter, though, and not as technical. In both letters Paul tries to make the point that God's grace, His love-no-matter-what-we've-done, is free for those who believe in him. It doesn't do any good to try to earn it. "Earning it" is not what Christianity is about. Christianity is about "believing it."

Ephesians

VITAL STATISTICS

Name: Ephesians. It was addressed to the people who lived in Ephesus.
When written: Around A.D. 60
Author: The apostle Paul. (He actually wrote this while he was imprisoned for his faith in Christ's deity.)
Kind of book: A letter of encouragement to a group, rather than one person
In a nutshell: This is the purpose of the church.
Place in the Bible: Fifth letter (Epistle) in the New Testament

AN ENCOURAGING WORD

The first part of the book of Ephesians is a lesson in encouragement. It is a wonderful reminder of God's love and grace. Some verses remind us of the truths of some of Paul's other letters:

> *For it is by grace you have been saved, through faith—*
> *and this is not from yourselves, it is the gift of God—*
> *not by works, so that no one can boast.*
> EPHESIANS 2:8–9

Other verses in Ephesians remind us that Paul was writing a letter of love to people for whom he cared deeply:

> *For this reason, ever since I heard about your faith in the Lord*
> *Jesus and your love for all God's people, I have not stopped*
> *giving thanks for you, remembering you in my prayers.*
> EPHESIANS 1:15–16

THE CHURCH

The last part of Ephesians focuses more specifically on the Church and how it can function best.

The Church should be a group of people in harmony.

 A FAITH IN SHINING ARMOR

The book of Ephesians gives a wonderful (and famous) word picture of how our faith equips us to face life. In Ephesians 6 Paul actually describes the Christian life in terms of pieces of armor.

- "Put on the full *armor of God*. . .so that when the day of evil comes, you may be able to stand your ground, and after you have done everything, to stand.
- Stand firm then, with the *belt of truth* buckled around your waist,
- with the *breastplate of righteousness* in place,
- and with your feet fitted with the readiness that comes from the *gospel of peace*.
- In addition to all this, take up the *shield of faith*, with which you can extinguish all the flaming arrows of the evil one.
- Take the *helmet of salvation* and
- the *sword of the Spirit*, which is the word of God.
- And pray in the Spirit on all occasions with all kinds of prayers and requests. With this in mind, be alert and always keep on praying for all the Lord's people" (Ephesians 6:11–18).

It always helps to have a word picture to help us understand how faith works. When we feel fragile, we can look down this list and examine our own lives to see what pieces of armor we need to oil and polish.

Philippians, Colossians

PHILIPPIANS

   VITAL STATISTICS

Name: Philippians. (It was written to the people in Philippi.)
When written: Around A.D. 60
Author: Paul the apostle. (He was in prison at the time.)
Kind of book: A personal letter, almost a thank-you note
In a nutshell: Joy really is possible with Jesus in your life, no matter what your circumstances are.
Place in the Bible: Sixth letter (Epistle) in the New Testament

BE JOYFUL

Philippians was a letter of joy. It was the kind of letter that had you smiling all the way back from the mailbox. On one hand, Paul wrote Philippians as a thank-you note for a financial gift. Leave it to Paul, though, to take the opportunity to give a little lesson with his thank-you.

Paul's lesson came first from his own life. He was chained to a Roman guard while he was writing, for goodness' sake! He was in jail. Yet he was writing about joy. What was his secret?

- Be a person of integrity (Philippians 1:27).
- Be humble and think about others before yourself (Philippians 2:3–4).
- Keep a positive attitude (Philippians 2:14).
- Remember what matters (Philippians 3:14).
- Learn to be content (Philippians 4:11–12).

"I have learned to be content whatever the circumstances. I know what it is to be in need, and I know what it is to have plenty. I have learned the secret of being content in any and every situation, whether well fed or hungry, whether living in plenty or in want" (Philippians 4:11–12).

COLOSSIANS

VITAL STATISTICS

Name: Colossians. (It was written to the church in Colossae.)
When written: Around A.D. 60
Author: Paul the apostle
Kind of book: A letter of correction
In a nutshell: Once again, Paul had to straighten out some heretical thinking.
Place in the Bible: Seventh letter (Epistle) in the New Testament
Key verse: *"Let the peace of Christ rule in your hearts, since as members of one body you were called to peace. And be thankful. . . . And whatever you do, whether in word or deed, do it all in the name of the Lord Jesus, giving thanks to God the Father through him"* (Colossians 3:15, 17).

Paul wrote to the Colossian Christians because they were falling prey to several heresies.

Worship: They may have been worshipping angels.
Legalism: They had come to believe that rules and regulations could make them righteous.
Arrogance: They were trusting their own goodness as opposed to God's.

Paul addressed these heresies and threw in some other wisdom just for good measure.

1 and 2 Thessalonians

1 THESSALONIANS

 VITAL STATISTICS

Name: 1 Thessalonians (the first of two letters written to the church in Thessalonica)
When written: Around A.D. 50
Author: Paul the apostle
Kind of book: A letter of instruction and encouragement to "keep your chin up"
In a nutshell: Christ will come again one day and life will be better.
Claim to fame: Some famous verses about Christ's second coming
Place in the Bible: Eighth letter (Epistle) in the New Testament
Key verse: *"Make it your ambition to lead a quiet life, to mind your own business and to work with your hands, just as we told you, so that your daily life may win the respect of outsiders and so that you will not be dependent on anybody" (1 Thessalonians 4:11–12).*

Being a Christian at the time this book was written was not a lot of fun. Today Christians wear cool T-shirts with spiritual sayings, and they attend large conferences where they learn more and more about the life they should live. Not so in Paul's day. Being a Christian was unpopular and even outlawed in some places. When someone became a Christian, they often had to leave their family behind and live in hiding. They needed all the encouragement they could get.

That's much of the reason Paul wrote to the Christians at Thessalonica. He couldn't make their situation any easier, and he couldn't promise them it wouldn't get worse before it got better. So he promised them the only thing he could. He promised them that one day Jesus would return and He would make things okay. In fact, this book has one of the most famous Bible passages about Jesus' return to the earth:

For the Lord himself will come down from heaven, with a loud command, with the voice of the archangel and with the trumpet call of God, and the dead in Christ will rise first. After that, we who are still alive and are left will be caught up together with them in the clouds to meet the Lord in the air. And so we will be with the Lord forever. Therefore encourage one another with these words. Now, brothers and sisters, about times and dates we do not need to write to you, for you know very well that the day of the Lord will come like a thief in the night.

1 THESSALONIANS 4:16–5:2

2 THESSALONIANS

 VITAL STATISTICS

Name: 2 Thessalonians (the second of two letters written to the church in Thessalonica)
When written: Around A.D. 50
Author: Paul (in fact, just a short time after he wrote 1 Thessalonians)
Kind of book: A letter of correction
In a nutshell: You need to be ready for Christ's coming, but that doesn't mean sitting in a lawn chair looking at the sky.
Place in the Bible: Ninth letter (Epistle) in the New Testament
Key verse: *"We hear that some among you are idle and disruptive. They are not busy; they are busybodies. Such people we command and urge in the Lord Jesus Christ to settle down and earn the food they eat" (2 Thessalonians 3:11–12).*

It was great for Paul to encourage the Thessalonian Christians in his first letter by reminding them that Jesus would come again to claim their victory. Paul didn't know, though, that they would take him sooooo literally. Some of them actually quit their jobs so they could watch for Christ. Others just started hanging out, looking for Christ's return. Still others got scared that

Jesus had already come and they had been left behind.

Now, it is true that we should all be ready for Christ's return as if it will be today. But when the bills come due, we need to be responsible to pay them. These Thessalonians weren't being responsible.

There was another problem, too. Since they didn't have anything to do and were bored, they began to do what people do when they are hanging out, bored. They began to make trouble, gossip, become busybodies, and get into everyone else's business. They began to mooch off one another because they had no money to pay their own bills.

That is why Paul wrote this second letter. He needed to pull them back to center, back to a balance.

"Concerning the coming of our Lord Jesus Christ and our being gathered to him, we ask you, brothers and sisters, not to become easily unsettled by the teaching allegedly from us—whether by a prophecy or by word of mouth or by letter—asserting that the day of the Lord has already come" (2 Thessalonians 2:1–2).

1 and 2 Timothy

1 TIMOTHY

 VITAL STATISTICS

Name: 1 Timothy. (Timothy was the young man to whom the letter was addressed.)
When written: About A.D. 65
Author: Paul, toward the end of his life
Kind of book: A very personal letter
In a nutshell: Don't let your youth stop you from living your life for God.
Claim to fame: Written specifically for young people of faith
Place in the Bible: Tenth letter (Epistle) in the New Testament
Key verse: *"Don't let anyone look down on you because you are young, but set an example for the believers in speech, in conduct, in love, in faith and in purity"* (1 Timothy 4:12).

Timothy was like an assistant or an apprentice to Paul. Perhaps he was even like a son to Paul. Paul wrote this letter to encourage Timothy, and to train him a little. It is a straightforward letter that is chock-full of advice for a young Christian (or any age Christian, really) who wants to please God with his or her life.

In this letter Paul covers some of the same ground that he touches on in other letters, such as

- worship,
- false teachers, and
- church leadership.

But he talks about them in a more personal way and with the urgency of an older man who wants to pour his years of experience into someone younger who can carry on the work.

Now the overseer [church leader] is to be above reproach,
faithful to his wife, temperate, self-controlled, respectable,
hospitable, able to teach, not given to drunkenness, not violent
but gentle, not quarrelsome, not a lover of money.
1 Timothy 3:2–3

But godliness with contentment is great gain. For we brought
nothing into the world, and we can take nothing out of it. But
if we have food and clothing, we will be content with that.
1 Timothy 6:6–8

VITAL STATISTICS

Name: 2 Timothy, named for the young man to whom it was addressed
When written: Around A.D. 65
Author: Paul the apostle, Timothy's teacher and friend
Kind of book: A personal letter, almost a good-bye letter
In a nutshell: Paul gives his final words to a dear friend and confidant.
Place in the Bible: Eleventh letter (Epistle) in the New Testament
Key verse: *"You then, my son, be strong in the grace that is in Christ Jesus. And the things you have heard me say in the presence of many witnesses entrust to reliable people who will also be qualified to teach others. Join with me in suffering, like a good soldier of Christ Jesus"* (2 Timothy 2:1–3).

Paul's second letter to Timothy is a poignant one. Paul knew that he was going to die. He was in prison. He had gone through several appeals. He knew that this was possibly his last letter to Timothy, his last chance to tell him the things that matter.

It is a wonderful thing that this letter is a part of the Bible. We are made privy to the most significant thoughts of one of the most famous preachers in the history of the world.

> *But as for you, continue in what you have learned and have become convinced of, because you know those from whom you learned it, and how from infancy you have known the holy Scriptures, which are able to make you wise for salvation through faith in Christ Jesus. All Scripture is God-breathed and is useful for teaching, rebuking, correcting and training in righteousness, so that the servant of God may be thoroughly equipped for every good work.*
> 2 TIMOTHY 3:14–17

For I am already being poured out like a drink offering, and the time for my departure is near. I have fought the good fight, I have finished the race, I have kept the faith.

2 TIMOTHY 4:6–7

Titus and Philemon

TITUS

 VITAL STATISTICS

Name: Titus, for the young pastor to whom it was addressed
When written: Around A.D. 65
Author: Paul the apostle
Type of book: A letter of instruction and training
In a nutshell: Paul wrote Titus specifically about choosing good leadership for the church in Crete.
Place in the Bible: Twelfth letter (Epistle) in the New Testament
Key verse: *"Since an overseer [church leader] manages God's household, he must be blameless—not overbearing, not quick-tempered, not given to drunkenness, not violent, not pursuing dishonest gain. Rather he must be hospitable, one who loves what is good, who is self-controlled, upright, holy and disciplined. He must hold firmly to the trustworthy message as it has been taught, so that he can encourage others by sound doctrine and refute those who oppose it"* (Titus 1:7–9).

Titus was a young pastor in a very difficult parish. He was a pastor in Crete, a small island south of Greece. The people of Crete were known for their lies, their laziness, and their cruelty. It was a place that needed a church, but was it a place in which you could find any leadership for the church?

This was the challenge before Titus. It was also one of the reasons Paul wrote so much to Titus about the qualities of a leader. Most churches still use Paul's criteria today when they are choosing their leaders (often called deacons or elders). The sad thing is, often today it is just as hard to find leaders who measure up.

> *For the grace of God has appeared that offers salvation to all people.*
> *It teaches us to say 'No' to ungodliness and worldly passions, and to*
> *live self-controlled, upright and godly lives in this present age.*
> Titus 2:11–12

> *But avoid foolish controversies and genealogies and arguments and*
> *quarrels about the law, because these are unprofitable and useless.*
> Titus 3:9

PHILEMON

VITAL STATISTICS

Name: Philemon, for the man who received the letter
When written: Around A.D. 60
Author: Paul the apostle
Type of book: A short note that almost functions as a letter of recommendation
In a nutshell: Paul asks a friend to forgive his runaway slave.
Place in the Bible: Thirteenth letter (Epistle) and the last letter by Paul in the New Testament

Paul's letter to Philemon is a unique letter in the New Testament. The basic story is that Philemon's slave Onesimus has run away and even stolen money from Philemon. While Onesimus is wandering, he becomes a Christian and comes in contact with Paul. Paul sends him home but with a letter hoping to soften Philemon's reaction. That letter is what we know as the book of Philemon.

Paul calls in a favor. He reminds Philemon that he has received from life and now it is time to give. Here is Paul's logic. . . .

"Although in Christ I could be bold and order you to do what you ought to do, yet I prefer to appeal to you on the basis of love" (Philemon 1:8–9). Paul appeals to Philemon's better self.

"So if you consider me a partner, welcome him as you would welcome me" (Philemon 1:17). Paul appeals to their friendship.

"I, Paul, am writing this with my own hand. . .not to mention that you owe me your very self" (Philemon 1:19). Paul is bordering on arm-twisting here.

"Confident of your obedience, I write to you, knowing that you will do even more than I ask" (Philemon 1:21). You always know you'd better come through when the person asking the favor thanks you ahead of time.

Hebrews

 VITAL STATISTICS

Name: Hebrews, which is another name for Jewish people or Israelites. Do you ever wonder, why all the names? The language is Hebrew, the nation descends from a man named Israel, and when Israel's land divided, the southern portion was Judah. Does that help?

When written: Around A.D. 70

Author: No one knows for sure, but a lot of people make guesses about it.

Type of book: A letter addressed to the Jewish people

In a nutshell: Hebrews is a well-thought-out argument to convince anyone listening that Jesus' life, death, and resurrection set a whole new standard of living superseding the Jewish law.

Place in the Bible: Fourteenth letter (Epistle) in the New Testament

Key verse: *"And without faith it is impossible to please God, because anyone who comes to him must believe that he exists and that he rewards those who earnestly seek him"* (Hebrews 11:6).

WHEN IT ALL BEGAN

Back when the Jewish nation was young, Moses wrote down the laws for the nation as God told them to him. (See Exodus and Leviticus if you need a refresher.) Some of these laws were VERY specific. As time passed and the Jewish people got more organized, some people made it their life's ambition to follow these laws. They concentrated so much on following the laws that sometimes they missed the point of having faith in God: loving God and loving others. They were too busy following rules and regulations to do that.

WHEN IT ALL CONTINUED

Jesus spent much of His energies addressing this kind of issue. We still address it today. Some people say, "I don't consider myself religious, but I'm a Christian." This usually means they believe they follow the heart of faith instead of the head of faith; that to them it's not just a bunch of dos and don'ts.

WHEN WILL IT ALL END?

Hebrews is addressing the same kind of thing. Some of the Jewish people were feeling like Jesus didn't make that much of a difference, that they could just keep following their laws and customs and that would make them righteous. The writer of Hebrews is saying to them, Jesus DID make a difference. He made all the difference. It's a whole different way of attaining righteousness—through faith in Christ, not in perfectly keeping the rules and making the sacrifices.

WHAT YOU FIND OUT ALONG THE WAY

Hebrews gives us some interesting insights into Jesus' role in our lives as a priest:

> *Therefore, since we have a great high priest who has ascended into heaven, Jesus the Son of God, let us hold firmly to the faith we profess. For we do not have a high priest who is unable to empathize with our weaknesses, but we have one who has been tempted in every way, just as we are—yet he did not sin. Let us then approach God's throne of grace with confidence, so that we may receive mercy and find grace to help us in our time of need.*
>
> HEBREWS 4:14–16

HALL OF FAITH

A lot of people call Hebrews 11 a "Hall of Fame" or a "Hall of Faith." How many of these people have you heard of?

- "By faith Abel. . .was commended as righteous. . . . And by faith Abel still speaks, even though he is dead.
- By faith Enoch. . .did not experience death.
- By faith Noah. . .built an ark to save his family. . .and became heir of the righteousness that is in keeping with faith.
- By faith Abraham. . .obeyed and went. . . . He made his home in the promised land. . .as did Isaac and Jacob, who were heirs with him of the same promise.
- By faith even Sarah, who was past childbearing age, was enabled to bear children.
- All these people were still living by faith when they died. They did not receive the things promised; they only saw them and welcomed them from a distance.
- By faith Abraham, when God tested him, offered Isaac as a sacrifice.
- By faith Isaac blessed Jacob and Esau in regard to their future.
- By faith Jacob, when he was dying, blessed each of Joseph's sons, and worshiped.
- By faith Joseph. . .spoke about the exodus of the Israelites from Egypt (this was before it happened).
- By faith Moses' parents hid him for three months. . .and they were not afraid of the king's edict.
- By faith Moses. . .persevered because he saw him who is invisible.
- By faith the people passed through the Red Sea as on dry land.
- By faith the walls of Jericho fell.
- By faith the prostitute Rahab. . .was not killed with those who were disobedient."

James

VITAL STATISTICS

Name: James, for the name of the author
When written: Probably around A.D. 50
Author: James, probably the half brother of Jesus
Type of book: A letter of instruction
In a nutshell: James is famous for his strong link between faith and good deeds. Does this sound familiar: "Faith without works is dead."
Place in the Bible: Fifteenth letter (Epistle) in the New Testament
Key verse: *"The wisdom that comes from heaven is first of all pure; then peace-loving, considerate, submissive, full of mercy and good fruit, impartial and sincere"* (James 3:17).

WHERE THE RUBBER MEETS THE ROAD

James is a practical book. It is a book that says not just what faith is, but what faith *does*. It is a book that explains not just what to believe, but how to live the life of a believer.

Even though James was probably written before Hebrews, it is a great book to come after Hebrews in the Bible. Hebrews is about faith. James is about faith applied.

James reminds us that being tempted and tested isn't the worst thing that could happen. He reminds us that listening is not enough without action. He reminds us that how we treat other people tells us the most about what we believe. He reminds us that what we say matters—a lot. He reminds us that the easy life isn't always the most nurturing environment for faith.

Here are some highlights of the kind of practical wisdom you'll find in the book of James.

How to communicate:

> *Everyone should be quick to listen, slow to speak and slow to become angry.*
> ### JAMES 1:19

What is the true test of our religion?

*Those who consider themselves religious and yet do not
keep a tight rein on their tongues deceive themselves,
and their religion is worthless.*

JAMES 1:26

 IMAGES THAT SPEAK

James is a good "describer." He uses visual images to show us truth
while he tells us truth. See if you can guess what James is describing.

What religion is worthless?
The religion of a person who can't control their tongue (James 1:26)

Who is blown by the wind and tossed by the sea?
*A person who asks for things from God but then doubts God will answer
(James 1:6)*

Who walks away from a mirror and forgets what his own face looks like?
A person who listens to God's word but doesn't do what it says (James 1:23)

What is like a body without a spirit?
Someone's faith without good deeds to back it up (James 2:26)

What is like the small rudder on a huge ship?
A person's tongue and the words they speak with it (James 3:4–5)

What is powerful and effective?
The prayer of a righteous person (James 5:16)

Who covers a multitude of sins?
The person who turns a sinner from their ways (James 5:20)

1 Peter

FINDING JOY

The book of 1 Peter was written at a time when many Christians were being persecuted. In fact, Christianity had been outlawed! Anyone who claimed to be a Christian could be tortured, imprisoned, and even killed simply because they believed in God and they believed that Jesus was God's Son.

You might think that if Peter was writing at such a volatile time he would have been depressed, or at least scared. When you read 1 Peter, though, you hear hope in Peter's message, not discouragement. You hear confidence, and if you listen really closely, you'll even hear joy. . . .

Praise be to the God and Father of our Lord Jesus Christ! In his great mercy he has given us new birth into a living hope through the resurrection of Jesus Christ from the dead.
1 PETER 1:3

Therefore, with minds that are alert and fully sober, set your
hope on the grace to be brought to you when Jesus Christ is
revealed at his coming.
1 PETER 1:13

But you are a chosen people, a royal priesthood, a holy nation,
God's special possession, that you may declare the praises of him
who called you out of darkness into his wonderful light. Once
you were not a people, but now you are the people of God; once
you had not received mercy, but now you have received mercy.
1 PETER 2:9–10

The end of all things is near. Therefore be alert and of sober
mind so that you may pray.
1 PETER 4:7

THAT'S AN INTERESTING POINT

First Peter raises two interesting issues for us to consider. First, civil disobedience. When do we stop obeying the laws of our culture in order to obey God? Peter reminds us over and over to give respect to our government in every way possible. He doesn't give us easy permission to ignore the laws of our land.

Also, persecution in the face of our innocence. The people to whom Peter was writing were not criminals. The thing they were being punished for was merely their faith. The sad truth of life is that we will face difficulties and mistreatment even when we don't deserve it. God's plan for us is not retribution. It is the ability to obey Him no matter what our circumstances. It is the ability to leave the "getting even" to God Himself.

2 Peter

SAME WRITER, DIFFERENT REASON

Peter wrote 2 Peter for a very different reason than he wrote 1 Peter. He wrote 1 Peter to address the unjust suffering many of his readers were facing. He was helping them combat enemies outside of the Church. On the other hand, in 2 Peter he was helping them combat enemies from inside the Church: false teachers.

Evidently, Peter had heard that the false teachers were telling the Church that Jesus wasn't REALLY coming back and that they wouldn't REALLY be accountable for their actions. These false teachers were exploiting their listeners and misleading many, many people.

DIFFERENT REASON, NEW BENEFITS

Because Peter was trying to "set the people straight" in light of false teaching, this short book has some of the New Testament's most bottom-line spiritual truth nuggets. It just works that way sometimes; you speak the most clearly when you are addressing a particular cause.

THE WORD OF GOD

Above all, you must understand that no prophecy of Scripture came about by the prophet's own interpretation of things. For prophecy never had its origin in the human will, but prophets, though human, spoke from God as they were carried along by the Holy Spirit.

2 PETER 1:20–21

GOD'S NATURE

The Lord is not slow in keeping his promise, as some understand slowness. Instead he is patient with you, not wanting anyone to perish, but everyone to come to repentance.

2 PETER 3:9

THE SECOND COMING OF CHRIST

But the day of the Lord will come like a thief. The heavens will disappear with a roar; the elements will be destroyed by fire, and the earth and everything done in it will be laid bare.

2 PETER 3:10

THE CHRISTIAN LIFE

For this very reason, make every effort to add to your faith goodness; and to goodness, knowledge; and to knowledge, self-control; and to self-control, perseverance; and to perseverance, godliness; and to godliness, mutual affection; and to mutual affection, love. For if you possess these qualities in increasing measure, they will keep you from being ineffective and unproductive in your knowledge of our Lord Jesus Christ.

2 PETER 1:5–8

WANTED!

Part of 2 Peter reads like a wanted poster for some very evil villains whom Peter calls "false teachers." Here are some of his juiciest descriptive phrases:

"They. . .secretly introduce destructive heresies. . . . In their greed these teachers will exploit you with fabricated stories. Their condemnation has long been hanging over them, and their destruction has not been sleeping" (2 Peter 2:1, 3).

"They are. . .unreasoning animals, creatures of instinct, born only to be caught and destroyed, and like animals they too will perish" (2 Peter 2:12).

"They are blots and blemishes" (2 Peter 2:13).

"They. . .never stop sinning. . .they are experts in greed" (2 Peter 2:14).

"These people are springs without water and mists driven by a storm. Blackest darkness is reserved for them" (2 Peter 2:17).

Do you think Peter had a problem with the teachers of false doctrine? Do you think this wanted poster could have said Dead or Alive?

1 John

VITAL STATISTICS

Name: 1 John, for the disciple who wrote it
When written: Around A.D. 90
Author: John, one of Jesus' disciples. (He also wrote the books of 2 and 3 John and Revelation.)
Type of book: A letter written to Christians to encourage and instruct them
In a nutshell: Living as children of God has to do with how we love and how we are loved.
Place in the Bible: Eighteenth letter (Epistle) of the New Testament and second book by John.

SETTING THE RECORD STRAIGHT

In some ways, John wrote this letter (which we call 1 John) as a way to set the record straight. No sooner had the early Church begun to organize itself than theological disagreements began. "Maybe Christ wasn't really human," said one group. "Maybe since Christ died for our sin, we don't have to try not to sin anymore," said another one. John wrote to respond to such ideas. "Yes," he said, "Jesus was fully human and fully God. Yes," he said, "We must fight our sinful natures with everything we have, but when we fall, there is forgiveness."

John wrote to warn the people against false teachings such as the ones above, as well as the false teachers who spread their very unholy curricula. He also wrote to instruct Christians in the way of love. John reminded his readers that the very evidence of God's presence in us and with us is our love for one another. Some of the most famous verses about love in the Bible are found in 1 John.

John wrote one of the most well-known verses about the love of God in his Gospel. Usually if people only know one verse in the Bible, they know

John 3:16: "For God so loved the world that he gave his one and only Son, that whoever believes in him shall not perish but have eternal life." Much of the book of 1 John is an expanded form of this idea. In fact, John almost restates John 3:16 in 1 John 4:9, "This is how God showed his love among us: He sent his one and only Son into the world that we might live through him."

John was a man who had laughed and talked and traveled with Jesus. He was one of Jesus' best friends. He should know, better than just about anyone, how to explain God's love to us.

TRUE LOVE

You want to know more about love? You can find out right here. Nope, it's not a talk show. It's not a dating game. It's a book of the Bible.

Love is what God is.
"And so we know and rely on the love God has for us. God is love. Whoever lives in love lives in God, and God in them" (1 John 4:16).

Being loved is being adopted.
"See what great love the Father has lavished on us, that we should be called children of God! And that is what we are!" (1 John 3:1).

Knowing God means loving others.
"Dear friends, let us love one another, for love comes from God. Everyone who loves has been born of God and knows God. Whoever does not love does not know God, because God is love" (1 John 4:7–8).

Being loved doesn't mean being afraid.
"There is no fear in love. But perfect love drives out fear" (1 John 4:18).

Loving God means obedience.
"This is love for God: to keep his commands" (1 John 5:3).

2 John, 3 John, Jude

2 JOHN

The Bible isn't a book like an encyclopedia. It isn't just full of facts. It is the record of God's actions and people's reactions. Second John is a good example of the personal nature of the Bible. It is a letter that John wrote either to an actual woman or to the Church (using "lady" as a metaphor). Either way, it is a very personal letter like one you might write to a friend going through a difficult time. What would you tell him or her? You'd say concentrate on what matters. Keep your chin up. Listen to the right people. That's what John did.

His command is that you walk in love.
2 JOHN 1:6

Anyone who runs ahead and does not continue
in the teaching of Christ does not have God.
2 JOHN 1:9

VITAL STATISTICS

Name: 3 John, the last of three letters written by John
When written: Around A.D. 90
Author: John, one of the twelve disciples
Type of book: A letter to a friend
In a nutshell: Make good choices. Keep helping people.
Claim to fame: One of the shortest books of the Bible with only
   fifteen verses
Place in the Bible: Twentieth letter (Epistle) in the New Testament
   and fourth book by John

3 John is an even more personal letter than 2 John. It is addressed to Gaius. This is what we know about Gaius—not much. The name Gaius is mentioned in the New Testament four times in association with the Church, but we have no idea whether these are all the same man or not. We know from this letter, though, that THIS Gaius was much loved and valued by John. We know that he was hospitable to traveling preachers like John and the apostle Paul. We know that Gaius was helpful. We can pretty easily assume that Gaius was a good person who was committed to following God and doing good things. He was the kind of person we would like to be. So what does John say to the kind of people we would like to be?

> *Dear friend, do not imitate what is evil but what is good.*
> *Anyone who does what is good is from God. Anyone who does*
> *what is evil has not seen God. . . . I hope to see you soon,*
> *and we will talk face to face.*
> 3 JOHN 1:11, 14

JUDE

If you had to describe the tone of the book of Jude, and if your only choices were (1) a party-type tone, (2) a business-type tone, or (3) an intense, big-brother-type tone, you would definitely choose number three: an intense, big-brother-type tone. Jude had something to say and he expected everyone to listen and to take it as seriously as he did.

Truthfully, what Jude said IS serious. He had spotted people who were destroying what God had created in the early Church. He wrote this book as if to say, "Not on my watch." Not only did these people teach false doctrine, but they destroyed fellowship, they deceived others, and they used people for their own means. They didn't get past Jude though. Thanks to his letter, they might not get past you either.

SLAM!

If you grew up in a rural area, you've probably heard some pretty good slams, like "He's lower than a snake's belly in a wagon rut." There's nothing like a colorful expression to put people in their place. Jude knew how to do that. Who would want to be on the receiving end of some of these?

- They're like people who pollute their own bodies.
- They're like blemishes at your love feasts.
- They're like shepherds who feed only themselves.
- They're like clouds without rain.
- They're like autumn trees, without fruit and uprooted—twice dead.
- They're like wild waves of the sea, foaming up their shame.
- They're like wandering stars, for whom blackest darkness has been reserved forever (Jude 1:8–13).

Aw, go on, Jude, tell us what you really think.

Revelation

VITAL STATISTICS

Name: Revelation, because it is based on a revelation (revealed truth, in this case a vision) that John the disciple had about the future

When written: Around A.D. 95

Author: John, a disciple, while he was living in exile on the island of Patmos

Type of book: A prophecy drawing the curtain back to let us see the anatomy of the end of the world

In a nutshell: John wrote this letter to describe the vision God gave him of the last days of the world as we know it.

Significance: There are other books of the Bible, even in the Old Testament, that include insights into the second coming of Christ and the end of the world. This book, though, is all about that topic.

Place in the Bible: Only book of Prophecy in the New Testament. Also it is the last book of the New Testament.

THE END OF THE WORLD AS WE KNOW IT

The bulk of the book of Revelation is about the end of the world, the apocalypse. In case you haven't noticed, a lot of people have spent a lot of energy preparing for, talking about, studying about, and just generally trying to figure out the details of the end of the world. One of the reasons it is so intriguing is that when the Bible talks about it, it is always in figurative language. It almost feels like a puzzle sometimes. While the Bible tells us Jesus will return like a thief when no one expects it, somehow we can't keep from trying to figure out just exactly when He'll return.

We have to remember, though, that the important thing about the "second coming of Christ" and the end of the world is the reminder to live each day honorably and connected with God, so that should this be our last day, it is a good one.

THE SEVEN CHURCHES

Before John's revelation goes into its wilder end-times images, Jesus gives simple messages to seven churches through John. For most of the messages Jesus gives both an affirmation and a warning. Here's a quick review of those messages:

The Church at Ephesus: You do the right things: you hate evil, you work hard, you persevere. But you've lost your first love. Put some heart back into your obedience (Revelation 2:1–7).

The Church at Smyrna: These are hard times for you and they are going to get harder. Be faithful and remember that your suffering won't last forever (Revelation 2:8–11).

The Church at Pergamum: You've remained true to God in an evil place, but you have not rid yourself of your evil influences. In this way you leave yourself at risk (Revelation 2:12–17).

The Church at Thyatira: You do many good things, but you let the people who teach lies continue to teach. How can you stand by and do nothing? (Revelation 2:18–29).

The Church at Sardis: Wake up! You are so lifeless. You have a few people who are true to Me, but you are a zombie as a church. I need you to pay attention (Revelation 3:1–6).

The Church at Philadelphia: You have been faithful. Keep persevering and I will protect you (Revelation 3:7–13).

The Church at Laodicea: You are complacent. You are hanging there in the middle. I'd rather you be hot or cold than just lukewarm (Revelation 3:14–22).

SPECIAL FX

After Jesus gives His charges to the churches, the rest of Revelation reads like a special effects display (or a sci-fi thriller, though this is certainly not fiction). John is in the midst of a vision of a whole different dimension than the one in which we live. He uses earthly images and language to give us as close a description as is possible. But how possible is it, really, to describe heaven in the language of earth? This is one of the main reasons why Revelation is so intriguing and yet so difficult to understand.

Basically, though, the end of the world will be a time when evil makes a last bid for people's allegiance through world leadership. There will be attempts to control our food, our loyalty, and our very survival, and it all will be somehow connected to where we place our faith. This is a big reason why people of faith get so uptight when the government tries to control their behavior in terms of their religious beliefs.

A REVELATION GLOSSARY OF TERMS

There are many different opinions about the order of the last events of our world. But most agree that there will be these common elements: An evil power will rise that eventually demands that the world worship him. Jesus will take believers from the earth. There will be some kind of brand or mark that will be required for people to buy or sell. There will be a great battle between Jesus and the evil world leader. Jesus will win and Satan will be defeated permanently. We will all give account for our lives.

Here are some terms you might have heard along the way.

666: We don't know exactly how this number will be used, but Revelation 13:18 does say that the number of the "beast" (part of the evil powerhead) will be 666. While no one is sure how the number will be used, everybody from movie producers to survivalists seems to know it's a number to stay away from.

Antichrist: The New Testament uses this term sometimes to mean any false teachers who try to influence people away from Christ, but in Revelation this term applies to a certain very powerful leader, probably with a political platform, who will be in power for three and a half years. He will eventually require the world to worship him and then will be defeated by Christ Himself.

Armageddon: the place of the final battle between Christ and the AntiChrist, between good and evil.

Heaven: Revelation promises a new heaven and a new earth. Heaven will be our home when the world as we know it is over and gone.

Last Judgment: This is when we will face God and give account for our lives. At this point it will matter most whether we have trusted Christ's death to cleanse us from sin, or whether we have mistakenly (and foolishly) trusted our own goodness to do that.

Millennium: A millennium is a thousand years. *The* Millennium in Revelation is the thousand years that Jesus will reign in peace. There are differing opinions as to *when* this millennium will happen in the order of "end-times" events.

Rapture: This is the onetime event when Jesus will immediately call all Christians home to heaven. Sometimes this term is used interchangeably with "the second coming of Christ."

Tribulation: This term refers to a time of terror and trouble for believers on earth. Some people believe this seven-year period will happen before Christ returns and the rapture occurs. Others believe it will happen after that.

INDEX